Disability

Editor: Tracy Biram

Volume 393

independence
educational publishers

First published by Independence Educational Publishers

The Studio, High Green

Great Shelford

Cambridge CB22 5EG

England

© Independence 2021

ISBN-13: 978 1 86168 851 4

Printed in Great Britain

Zenith Print Group

Contents

Introduction

Disability is Volume 393 in the **issues** series. The aim of the series is to offer current, diverse information about important issues in our world, from a UK perspective.

ABOUT DISABILITY

The term 'disability' covers a wide range of physical, psycho-social or sensory impairments which may or may not affect a person's ability to carry out their day-to-day activities. This book looks at the challenges faced by people living with disabilities, such as: discrimination, representation, accessibilty issues and availability of social care, particularly in the UK.

OUR SOURCES

Titles in the **issues** series are designed to function as educational resource books, providing a balanced overview of a specific subject.

The information in our books is comprised of facts, articles and opinions from many different sources, including:

♦ Newspaper reports and opinion pieces

♦ Website factsheets

♦ Magazine and journal articles

♦ Statistics and surveys

♦ Government reports

♦ Literature from special interest groups.

A NOTE ON CRITICAL EVALUATION

Because the information reprinted here is from a number of different sources, readers should bear in mind the origin of the text and whether the source is likely to have a particular bias when presenting information (or when conducting their research). It is hoped that, as you read about the many aspects of the issues explored in this book, you will critically evaluate the information presented.

It is important that you decide whether you are being presented with facts or opinions. Does the writer give a biased or unbiased report? If an opinion is being expressed, do you agree with the writer? Is there potential bias to the 'facts' or statistics behind an article?

ASSIGNMENTS

In the back of this book, you will find a selection of assignments designed to help you engage with the articles you have been reading and to explore your own opinions. Some tasks will take longer than others and there is a mixture of design, writing and research-based activities that you can complete alone or in a group.

FURTHER RESEARCH

At the end of each article we have listed its source and a website that you can visit if you would like to conduct your own research. Please remember to critically evaluate any sources that you consult and consider whether the information you are viewing is accurate and unbiased.

Useful Websites

www.bighack.org

www.bylinetimes.com

www.cambridge-news.co.uk

www.dibservices.org.uk

www.disabilityhorizons.com

www.disabilityunit.blog.gov.uk

www.equalityhumanrights.com

www.humanity-inclusion.org.uk

www.independent.co.uk

www.leonardcheshire.org

www.mencap.org.uk

www.scope.org.uk

www.shoutoutuk.org

www.telegraph.co.uk

www.theconversation.com

www.theguardian.com

www.who.int

Definitions of disability

The social model of disability

We encourage the use of the social model as a way of understanding disability. It says that disability is created by barriers in society.

The barriers generally fall into 3 categories:

♦ the environment – including inaccessible buildings and services

♦ people's attitudes – stereotyping, discrimination and prejudice

♦ organisations – inflexible policies, practices and procedures

The issue is the 'disabling environment' and the negative attitudes towards disability.

Disability is caused by an unaccommodating environment, negative attitudes and organisational structures:

♦ Inaccessible transport

♦ Poorly designed buildings

♦ Segregated services

♦ Stereotyping

♦ Lack of understanding

♦ Too few sign language interpreters

Definition of disability under the Equality Act 2010

You're disabled under the Equality Act 2010 if you have a physical or mental impairment that has a 'substantial' and 'long-term' negative effect on your ability to do normal daily activities.

What 'substantial' and 'long-term' mean

♦ 'substantial' is more than minor or trivial - e.g. it takes much longer than it usually would to complete a daily task like getting dressed

♦ 'long-term' means 12 months or more - e.g. a breathing condition that develops as a result of a lung infection

There are special rules about recurring or fluctuating conditions, for example, arthritis.

The medical model of disability

The standard way of thinking about disability in the past was the so-called Medical Model.

The issue is the individual with a condition/impairment

Disability is caused by conditions/impairments which people have, e.g.

♦ Is housebound

♦ Needs help to do things

♦ Confined to a wheelchair

♦ Can't walk

♦ Requires medication

♦ Depends on a hearing aid

♦ Has difficulty understanding

Disability: the global picture

One billion people around the world live with some form of disability, making up around 15% of the global population. The vast majority of people with disabilities live in developing countries.

According to the World Report on Disability, the number of people with disabilities is increasing. This is because populations are ageing (older people have a higher risk of disability) and because of the global increase in chronic health conditions associated with disability, such as diabetes, cardiovascular diseases and mental illness. Other environmental factors, such as road accidents, natural disasters and conflicts also contribute to the increase in disability.

Despite being "the world's biggest minority", people with disabilities are often forgotten. They regularly face discrimination and exclusion from water and sanitation, healthcare, education, work, and community life. And even though disabled people are among the poorest and most vulnerable, their needs are often overlooked by governments and by international organisations. Efforts to reduce poverty can only be effective if we include people with disabilities!

Vicious circle of poverty and disability

Disability is both a cause and a consequence of poverty: poor people are more likely to become disabled, and people with disabilities are among the poorest of the poor. This relationship can be seen as a vicious circle, with poverty leading to disability and disability worsening poverty.

The main links between poverty and disability are:

♦ Dangerous and unhealthy living conditions, such as inadequate housing, water and sanitation, and unsafe transportation and work conditions.

♦ The absence or inaccessibility of medical care or rehabilitation. People with disabilities are confronted with extra costs related to disability such as personal assistance, healthcare or assistive devices. These additional costs increase their risk of being poorer than others.

♦ Limited access to education and employment. People with disabilities are more likely to be unemployed and are generally paid less when they are employed.

♦ Social exclusion: People with disabilities often do not have access to public spaces because of physical barriers, and often cannot participate in political decision-making, meaning that their voices are not heard and their needs are overlooked.

Double discrimination

Disability covers a great variety of situations and people with disabilities are not a homogeneous group. There are significant inequalities, and poor people, women, and old people are more likely to experience disability than others.

For example, women and girls with disabilities experience double discrimination on account of their gender and their disability, and are also particularly vulnerable to violence and abuse.

School enrolment rates also differ among impairments: children with physical impairments generally fare better than those with intellectual or sensory impairments.

Those most excluded from the labour market are often those with mental health issues or learning disabilities. People with more severe impairments often experience greater disadvantage.

The above information is reprinted with kind permission from Humanity & Inclusion.
© 2021 Humanity & Inclusion UK

www.humanity-inclusion.org.uk

Autism spectrum disorders

Key facts

♦ Autism spectrum disorders (ASD) are a diverse group of conditions. Characteristics of autism may be detected in early childhood, but autism is often not diagnosed until much later.

♦ About one in 160 children has an ASD (1).

♦ The abilities and needs of people with autism vary and can evolve over time.

♦ While some people with autism can live independently, others have severe disabilities and require life-long care and support.

♦ Evidence-based psychosocial interventions can improve communication and social skills, with a positive impact on the well-being and quality of life of people with autism and also their caregivers.

♦ People with autism are often subject to stigma, discrimination and human rights violations.

♦ Care for people with autism needs to be accompanied by actions at community and societal levels for greater accessibility, inclusivity and support.

Introduction

Autism spectrum disorders (ASD) are a diverse group of conditions. They are characterised by some degree of difficulty with social interaction and communication.

Other characteristics are atypical patterns of activities and behaviours, such as difficulty with transition from one activity to another, a focus on details and unusual reactions to sensations.

The abilities and needs of people with autism vary and can evolve over time. While some people with autism can live independently, others have severe disabilities and require life-long care and support. Autism often has an impact on education and employment opportunities. In addition, the demands on families providing care and support can be significant. Societal attitudes and the level of support provided by local and national authorities are important factors determining the quality of life of people with autism.

Characteristics of autism may be detected in early childhood, but autism is often not diagnosed until much later.

People with autism often have co-occurring conditions, including epilepsy, depression, anxiety and attention deficit hyperactivity disorder as well as challenging behaviours such as difficulty sleeping and self-injury. The level of intellectual functioning among people with autism varies widely, extending from profound impairment to superior levels.

Epidemiology

It is estimated that worldwide about one in 160 children has an ASD. This estimate represents an average figure, and reported prevalence varies substantially across studies.

Some well-controlled studies have, however, reported figures that are substantially higher. The prevalence of ASD in many low- and middle-income countries is unknown.

Causes

Available scientific evidence suggests that there are probably many factors that make a child more likely to have an ASD, including environmental and genetic factors.

Available epidemiological data conclude that there is no evidence of a causal association between measles, mumps and rubella vaccine, and ASD. Previous studies suggesting a causal link were found to be filled with methodological flaws(2)(3).

There is also no evidence to suggest that any other childhood vaccine may increase the risk of ASD. Evidence reviews of the potential association between the preservative thiomersal and aluminium adjuvants contained in inactivated vaccines and the risk of ASD strongly concluded that vaccines do not increase the risk of ASD.

Assessment and care

A broad range of interventions, from early childhood and across the life span, can optimize the development, health, well-being and quality of life of people with autism.

Timely access to early evidence-based psychosocial interventions can improve the ability of children with autism to communicate effectively and interact socially. The monitoring of child development as part of routine maternal and child health care is recommended.

It is important that, once autism has been diagnosed, children, adolescents and adults with autism and their carers are offered relevant information, services, referrals, and practical support, in accordance with their individual and evolving needs and preferences.

The health-care needs of people with autism are complex and require a range of integrated services, that include health promotion, care and rehabilitation.

Collaboration between the health sector and other sectors, particularly education, employment and social care, is important.

Interventions for people with autism and other developmental disabilities need to be designed and delivered with the participation of people living with these conditions.

Care needs to be accompanied by actions at community and societal levels for greater accessibility, inclusivity and support.

Human rights

All people, including people with autism, have the right to the enjoyment of the highest attainable standard of physical and mental health.

And yet, people with autism are often subject to stigma and discrimination, including unjust deprivation of health care, education and opportunities to engage and participate in their communities.

People with autism have the same health problems as the general population. However, they may, in addition, have specific health-care needs related to ASD or other co-occurring conditions. They may be more vulnerable to developing chronic noncommunicable conditions because of behavioural risk factors such as physical inactivity and poor dietary preferences, and are at greater risk of violence, injury and abuse.

People with autism require accessible health services for general health-care needs like the rest of the population, including promotive and preventive services and treatment of acute and chronic illness. Nevertheless, people with autism have higher rates of unmet health-care needs compared with the general population. They are also more vulnerable during humanitarian emergencies. A common barrier is created by healthcare providers' inadequate knowledge and understanding of autism.

WHO Resolution on autism spectrum disorders (WHA67.8)

In May 2014, the Sixty-seventh World Health Assembly adopted a resolution entitled "Comprehensive and coordinated efforts for the management of autism spectrum disorders (ASD)," which was supported by more than 60 countries.

The resolution urges WHO to collaborate with Member States and partner agencies to strengthen national capacities to address ASD and other developmental disabilities.

WHO response

WHO and partners recognize the need to strengthen countries' abilities to promote the optimal health and well-being of all people with autism.

WHO's efforts focus on:

♦ increasing the commitment of governments to taking action to improve the quality of life of people with autism;

♦ providing guidance on policies and action plans that address autism within the broader framework of health, mental health and disabilities;

♦ contributing to strengthening the ability of caregivers and the health workforce to provide appropriate and effective care for people with autism; and

♦ promoting inclusive and enabling environments for people with autism and other developmental disabilities.

References
(1) Mayada et al. Global prevalence of autism and other pervasive developmental disorders. Autism Res. 2012 Jun; 5(3): 160–179.
(2) Wakefield's affair: 12 years of uncertainty whereas no link between autism and MMR vaccine has been proved. Maisonneuve H, Floret D. Presse Med. 2012 Sep; French (https://www.ncbi.nlm.nih.gov/pubmed/22748860).
(3) Lancet retracts Wakefield's MMR paper. Dyer C. BMJ 2010;340:c696. 2 February 2010 (https://www.bmj.com/content/340/bmj.c696.long).

1 June 2021

What is a learning disability?

Learning disabilites: our definition

A learning disability is a reduced intellectual ability and difficulty with everyday activities – for example household tasks, socialising or managing money – which affects someone for their whole life.

People with a learning disability tend to take longer to learn and may need support to develop new skills, understand complicated information and interact with other people.

What learning disability means

We asked people with a learning disability what learning disability means to them.

It's important to remember that with the right support, most people with a learning disability in the UK can lead independent lives.

Learning disability support

The level of support someone needs depends on the individual.

For example, someone with a mild learning disability may only need support with things like getting a job. However, someone with a severe or profound learning disability may need full time care and support with every aspect of their life – they may also have physical disabilities.

People with certain specific conditions can have a learning disability too. For example, people with Down's syndrome and some people with autism have a learning disability.

Learning difficulties?

Learning disability is often confused with learning difficulties such as dyslexia or ADHD. Mencap describes dyslexia as a "learning difficulty" because, unlike learning disability, it does not affect intellect.

Different types of learning disability

There are different types of learning disability, which can be mild, moderate, severe or profound. In all cases a learning disability is lifelong.

It can be difficult to diagnose a mild learning disability as the individual will often mix well with others and will be able to cope with most everyday tasks. However, they may need support in other areas of their life such as filling out forms.

People with a severe learning disability or profound and multiple learning disability (PMLD) will need more care and support with areas such as mobility, personal care and communication. People with a moderate learning disability may also need support in these areas, but not definitely.

For any parent, the greatest concern will be your child's wellbeing and their future. As a parent, you can help your child by encouraging their strengths and getting the right support to help them overcome the things they find difficult. Every child is an individual with their own needs, but with the right support children with a learning disability can lead fulfilling lives in the way they choose.

What can cause a learning disability?

A learning disability occurs when the brain is still developing (before, during or soon after birth). Several things can cause a learning disability.

Before birth things can happen to the central nervous system (the brain and spinal cord) that can cause a learning disability. A child can be born with a learning disability if the mother has an accident or illness while she is pregnant, or if the unborn baby develops certain genes.

Genes are chemicals in our bodies that contain information about us, like how we look.

A person can be born with a learning disability if he or she does not get enough oxygen during childbirth, has trauma to the head, or is born too early.

After birth, a learning disability can be caused by early childhood illnesses, accidents and seizures.

Getting a diagnosis

A learning disability can be diagnosed at any time. A child may be diagnosed at birth, or you might notice a difference in your child's development during early childhood. For some people it may be many years before they receive a diagnosis, while others may never receive a diagnosis at all.

Although getting a diagnosis can be a very difficult and emotional experience, it is often the first step to accessing the care and support needed for the future.

Accessibility and disability: facts and figures

Research and statistics into disability, accessibility and the spending power of disabled people.

By Elisabeth Ward

We often use lots of statistics from Scope and other research to help us show

- why accessibility is important
- how it affects disabled people
- the barriers disabled people face

But it can be a lot of work to collect that information together. Where do you start looking? We want to make it easy to share stats that will:

- explain why your organisation needs to do accessibility
- show how many of your potential customers might be disabled
- help us raise awareness about accessibility

We've collected together what we think are important and useful statistics. You can share them with your colleagues, clients, customers and anyone else you think they can support.

Our disabled population

Here are some statistics on how many people are disabled in the UK:

- 14.1 million disabled people, that's 1 in 5 people
- 19% of working age adults are disabled

- 44% of pension age adults are disabled
- 40% of households have at least 1 disabled person

Sources: Family Resources Survey 2016/17; Scope analysis of ONS Family Resources Survey 2018/19

Different impairments and conditions

Digital inaccessibility can affect a range of people and create barriers.

It's important to understand the different ways disabled people access digital products.

Whether that's:

- using a screen reader
- tabbing through with a keyboard
- needing plain English to understand information
- using captions for videos

Accessibility is not just designing for one impairment or condition. It's designing inclusively to meet a range of needs.

So here are some stats on how many people in the UK have specific conditions and impairments:

- around 1.5 million people have a learning difficulty
- estimated 1 in 10 people have dyslexia
- estimated 2 million people are living with sight loss

- 12 million have hearing loss greater than 25dBHL

- estimated 151,000 people use British Sign Language

Sources: How common is a learning disability? (Mencap)
Dyslexia (NHS)
Key information and statistics on sight loss in the UK (RNIB)
Facts and figures (RNID)

Attitudes to disability

Attitudes to disability affect how people think about accessibility. And how much they care about inclusion.

- 60% of people underestimate how many disabled people there actually are

- 75% of people think of disabled people in general as needing to be cared for

- 32% think disabled people are not as productive as non-disabled people

- 13% hardly ever or never think of disabled people as the same as everyone else

It's important to change attitudes to inspire social change and an inclusive working culture. Disabled people have so much untapped potential due to other people's attitudes.

"We spend our lives cultivating an intuitive creativity because we are forced to navigate a world that isn't built for our bodies." - Liz Jackson, Disabled List

We should not be forced to navigate a world full of unnecessary barriers.

Unsurprisingly, how non-disabled people view disability affects how disabled people feel:

- 49% of working age adults feel excluded from society because of their condition or impairment

- 41% of working age disabled people do not feel valued by society

Sources: Scope Disability perception gap report; Scope Gamechangers campaign

Access to digital technology and services

Digital technology and access to online services can be essential for disabled people to live independently:

"78% of disabled people say that having access to digital technologies is helpful or very helpful."

Unfortunately, digital and online barriers stop disabled people accessing information, products, services, and apps.

- disabled people are over 50% more likely to face barriers to accessing digital and online services than non-disabled people

- if you have an impairment you are 3 times more likely not to have the skills to access devices and get online

The WebAIM annual accessibility analysis of the top 1 million homepages shows that Web Content Accessibility Guidelines (WCAG) errors are slowly going up. Businesses need to do more to change this and become more accessible.

The 2021 analysis shows that 97.4% of homepages had detectable accessibility errors. This is down slightly from 98.1% in February 2020.

The 5 most common WCAG failures were:

- Low contrast – 86% of homepages

- Missing alt text for images – 61% of homepages

- Empty links – 51% of homepages

- Missing form input labels – 54% of homepages

- Empty buttons – 27% of homepages

Sources: Scope Independent, confident, connected report; Reason Digital radical accessibility via Populus; Lloyds Bank UK Consumer Digital Index 2020; The WebAIM Million, February 2020

The spending power of disabled people

The collective spending power of disabled people and their household continues to grow.

It's estimated to be worth £274 billion per year to UK business.

The research also showed how much industry lost by not being accessible:

- High street shops – £267 million

- Restaurants, pubs and clubs – £163 million

- Supermarkets – £501 million

- Energy companies – £44 million

- Phone and internet providers – £49 million

- Transport providers – £42 million

- Banks or building societies – £935 million

Source: Purple pound

Financial loss to businesses

Businesses lose money from disabled customers due to inaccessible websites and products. In 2016, research showed that:

- 7 in 10 disabled customers said they will click away from a website that they find difficult to use

- 4 million people abandoned a retail website because of the barriers

- an estimated loss of £11.75 billion from the 'Click-Away Pound'

In 2019, the Click-Away Pound has grown to £17.1 billion.

According to Accenture's analysis of the Disability Equality Index (DEI), companies that prioritise digital inclusion:

- are twice as likely to have higher shareholder returns

- 28% higher revenue

♦ see a 30% better performance in economic profit margins

The DEI is a tool that gives US businesses an objective score based on their disability inclusion policies and practices.

Sources: Click-away pound report 2016. Click-away pound 2019. The Disability Inclusion Advantage, Accenture (PDF)

Main barriers within organisations

The biggest barriers to adopting accessibility within an organisation include:

♦ Lack of clear ownership within the organisation – 43%

♦ Lack of 'the right people or skills' – 16%

♦ Finding it hard to justify the spend – 11%

♦ Not sure what accessibility actually means – 10%

♦ Senior leadership not convinced of the benefits – 6%

The top 2 incentives for becoming accessible:

♦ Universal benefits of accessibility – 52%

♦ Avoiding legal action – 27%

And a huge 65% of organisations have not tested their websites with real disabled people.

Findings based on the responses of more than 100 UK digital professionals.

Source: Digital Accessibility: Achieving Great CX For All (Inviqa)

14 April 2021

Living with non-visible disabilities

Government Disability Unit blogpost.

What is a non-visible disability?

A non-visible disability is a disability or health condition that is not immediately obvious.

It can defy stereotypes of what people might think disabled people look like.

This can make it difficult for people with non-visible disabilities to access what they need.

The impact of living with a non-visible disability can be slight, or can have a huge effect on someone's life.

Why is it called a non-visible disability?

Many disabled people self-identify in different ways. There are several ways of talking about non-visible disabilities.

Some people with disabilities that are not obvious prefer the phrase 'non-visible'. This is because the word 'invisible' can erase the legitimacy of the disability, or imply the disability does not exist.

'Hidden' disability can imply a person is hiding their disability on purpose. 'Less-visible' disability does not encompass those whose condition is completely non-visible.

With non-visible disabilities it is important to emphasise that even though the disability cannot be seen, it does not mean it does not exist.

Some 'non-visible' conditions are visible or obvious sometimes. Also, they can be 'seen' by some people who might have a better understanding of the condition. But they are not usually visible to others.

Non-visible disabilities are named this way because you cannot always easily see the nature of the disability. Some people with non-visible disabilities might use mobility aids, whereas others will not.

Also, some people with non-visible disabilities might have a 'dynamic disability'. This means that sometimes they might use a mobility aid, but other times they might not need it. Likewise, sometimes they might need to use a priority seat on busy public transport.

Other times they may not feel they need to.

Which disabilities are non-visible?

Daily life can look different for people with non-visible disabilities. Non-visible disabilities include a wide range of disabilities. These are not limited to, but may include:

♦ mental health conditions, including anxiety, depression, schizophrenia, personality disorders, obsessive compulsive disorder

♦ autism and Asperger's syndrome visual impairments or restricted vision

♦ hearing loss

♦ sensory and processing difficulties

♦ cognitive impairment, including dementia, traumatic brain injury, or learning disabilities

♦ non-visible health conditions, including diabetes, chronic pain or fatigue, respiratory conditions, incontinence

There are many different types of non-visible disability. The kind of support that people with non-visible disabilities need differs.

It is best not to assume what kind of support someone might need. Listening to the needs of disabled people and acting on them is the best course of action.

How should I act towards people with non-visible disabilities?

People with non-visible disabilities want to be treated with respect and as individuals – just like people with visible disabilities and the general population. Even though you cannot see evidence of a disability, the disability still exists.

Nobody has to tell you they have a disability, or explain what it is. People can choose to keep this private. Some people may choose to wear a lanyard or carry a badge to show that they have a non-visible disability. It shows they may need extra support whilst travelling or shopping. Other people with non-visible disabilities prefer not to do this. Some people may wear a different lanyard or badge to alert you to their disability or 'impairment'.

Non-visible disabilities and COVID-19

Some people with non-visible disabilities are more vulnerable or susceptible to COVID-19, but others are not. Some people with non-visible disabilities are exempt from wearing face-coverings.

If you are exempt, you do not have to prove this to other people. Some people who have exemptions and a non-visible disability want to demonstrate that they are exempt.

There are several schemes which allow someone to do this. You could wear the sunflower lanyard or cards explaining you have a medical exemption from wearing a face-covering.

Schemes include:

♦ GOV.UK exemption templates

♦ Sunflower Lanyard

♦ RNIB

♦ Macular Society

♦ National Autism Society

♦ Independent Living UK

There are many other organisations and disability charities that produce bespoke mask-exemption identification.

Raising awareness

We can provide better support the more we understand about non-visible illnesses.

Everyday things can be difficult for people with non-visible disabilities. These include travel, work, shopping and socialising.

Making sure not to judge someone based on whether their disability is visible or not is crucial.

Listening to disabled people and making sure accessibility is inclusive is important. This could help improve the lives of people with non-visible disabilities.

17 December 2020

Neglected, hidden away, registered dead: the tragic true story of the Queen's disabled cousins

An episode in the new series of *The Crown* sheds light on a little-known – and long-obscured – stain upon the Royal family's reputation.

By Susannah Goldsbrough

*T*he Crown turns a colder eye on the Royal family this season than it has in any previous period. Two prominent new personalities – Diana, Princess of Wales and Margaret Thatcher – are thrust into the limelight, and the treatment they receive at the hands of "The Firm" will leave many viewers recoiling at the unkindness and snobbery.

But perhaps the most damning portrayal so far of the Royals by *Crown* writer Peter Morgan – who is usually sympathetic towards them – comes in the episode telling the story of Nerissa and Katherine Bowes-Lyon.

The third and fifth daughters of John and Fenella Bowes-Lyon – John being the elder brother of Queen Elizabeth, the Queen Mother – both women were born with severe developmental disabilities. Neither learned to talk. Their medical diagnosis is revealing of contemporary attitudes towards such conditions: officially, they were "imbeciles".

In 1941, when Nerissa was 22 years old and Katherine 15, the family had them committed to the Royal Earlswood Hospital, in Redhill, Surrey, apparently on medical advice. Three of their cousins, Idonea, Rosemary and Ethelreda, the children of Fenella's sister, were similarly disabled and sent to the same hospital.

Earlswood was the first purpose-built facility of its kind, but it was not a happy place. Nurses and relatives of former inmates, interviewed in 2011 as part of a Channel 4 documentary about the sisters, recalled an institution that was regimented and devoid of fun. There were wards of up to 40 people, cared for by two nurses. "You gave them a bath, cut their nails, fed them if they needed help," one recalled.

The Bowes-Lyon sisters seem to have been entirely abandoned by the Royal family, aside from the £125 a year they paid Earlswood. According to the programme, nobody – not even the women's parents – ever visited, or remembered their birthdays, or sent them Christmas cards. Speaking to Thames News in 1987, a hospital representative said of Nerissa: "She was last visited, so far as I'm aware, by direct relatives in the early 1960s."

In 1963, the family's entry in Burke's Peerage declared that both daughters were dead. This was made more poignant

by their apparent awareness of their royal connections – as *The Crown* misses no opportunity to ram home: we see them with photographs of Elizabeth and Margaret kept lovingly framed by their bedsides and curtseying and saluting whenever the family appeared on television. Nurses recall their excitement at the wedding of Charles and Diana.

How involved the inner circle of the Royal family were in their treatment remains unclear.

The Crown suggests that by the 1980s, Nerissa and Katherine had been all but forgotten.

Princess Margaret stumbles across the fact of their existence entirely accidentally, via her own therapist, while the Queen, apparently a religious reader of Burke's, believes them both to have passed away.

Is this too generous a depiction? Nerissa and Katherine were, after all, their first cousins. It is even more difficult to believe that the Queen Mother was not aware or complicit in the stashing away of two of her brother's children. When Margaret confronts her in *The Crown*, she does not attempt to deny it; indeed, she is defiant. "Don't be so naive," she tells Margaret, in response to her accusations of cruelty. "We had no choice."

(In a note of sour irony, the Queen Mother was a patron of the Royal Mencap Society, a charity working for people with disabilities.)

What has never been cleared up is the family's motivation for its treatment of Nerissa and Katherine. How far was it a cruel but conventional reaction to disability at a time when it was extremely poorly understood, and how far a cold, calculating political strategy to protect the Windsors' hold on the crown? Certainly, the existence of the false report of their deaths in Burke's has the bitter flavour of a royal cover-up.

Peter Morgan makes no attempt to hide his belief in the more chilling interpretation. His fictionalised Queen Mother effectively confesses to masterminding the entire arrangement:

"The idea that one family alone has the automatic birthright to the crown is already so hard to justify," she tells Margaret. "The gene pool of that family had better have 100 per cent purity." The girls were sent to Earlswood just four years after Edward VIII's abdication put the children of a Bowes-Lyon in the direct line of succession.

The Queen Mother also mentions Prince John, the youngest son of George V, brother to George VI and Edward VIII, in her explanation of the family's actions. The Windsor side alone already had enough "examples" to worry people, she says. John was diagnosed with epilepsy at the age of three. When his condition deteriorated, he was sent to live on a secluded corner of the Sandringham estate with a nanny, away from the public eye – and the family. He died there at the age of 13, following a severe seizure.

The Crown's Margaret is, perhaps implausibly, concerned about the implications of the existence of the sisters for her own chances of developing mental health problems. It is a plot device that allows her therapist to reveal that Nerissa and Katherine's conditions were genetically inherited from their mother's side and so could not conceivably affect the Windsor bloodline. The existence of the two women's three disabled cousins proves the point. Nonetheless, Margaret concludes, "what my family did was unforgivable."

Nerissa died in 1986 and was buried in Redhill Cemetery. Only hospital staff attended her funeral and her grave was marked with plastic tags and a serial number. But Katherine lived on, and when the story broke in 1987, people from all across Britain sent her flowers.

Descendants of the Bowes-Lyons, meanwhile, tried to defend the actions of the Royal family. Fenella's great-nephew, Lord Clinton, told the press that the official death report must have been an accident; Fenella, who handled the Burke's forms, was "a very vague person". Accidentally providing false death dates for two of your children was, he seemed to imply, easily done.

At the time, Buckingham Palace said the Queen was aware of the report, but had no comment on the matter. "It's a matter for the Bowes-Lyon family," a representative said.

15 November 2020

I am a proud disability activist but know almost nothing about the history of our movement – it is time for change

Disabled people are not a monolith and our stories and history deserve to be told, so that the next generation of disabled activists are not left in the dark.

By Shona Louise

I have been a proud disability activist for almost five years now, using my voice to speak up about everything from the plastic straw ban to access on public transport and inaccessibility in theatres. But despite my strong identity as a disabled person, I am ashamed to admit I know little of my own history.

As Disability History Month approaches in the UK I've been thinking more and more about how many gaps there are in my knowledge of disability rights and the battles fought to afford me the rights I have today. My activism has been so focused on the here and now, and on fighting for a better future, that I've spent little time educating myself on what led us here. And it is me having to educate myself – because this isn't something they teach in schools.

The history I know has been picked up from older disabled people via social media over the years and is compiled of knowing that the Disability Discrimination Act existed before the current Equality Act, and that at some point disabled people chained themselves to buses to achieve equal access. I wouldn't exactly call that a wealth of knowledge. The more I dwell on how little I know, and the less I honour the struggles of previous generations, the more ashamed I am to call myself an activist.

It was the release of Netflix's Crip Camp, a documentary about a summer camp for teens with disabilities, that had me first confronting my lack of awareness. I remember seeing tweets from non-disabled people saying they had no idea about America's disability history; I also remember sharing those feelings.

Whether you are born disabled or acquire a disability later in life, no one hands you a guide or a manual on how to navigate life. No one teaches you about your history and so we are left to fill in the gaps ourselves. I'm a big believer that we need to know where we've come from, so we can look towards the future.

Of course there is a danger that looking back provides an excuse not to strive for more.

Comments like, "Look how far we've come" or "20 years ago you wouldn't be able to do the things you do today" should not be used as a reason to compromise. There is a culture of disabled people having to be grateful for whatever they are given in society and comments like these contribute to that.

I want to fight this culture while still celebrating the people and movements that got me where I am today. I want to honour the individuals who laid the foundations for the work that myself and other disability activists are currently doing. Finding this information is not easy, though; I look at other equal rights movements and I know who the prominent figures are but finding the names of the revolutionaries who kickstarted the disability rights movement is a lot harder.

During previous efforts to learn more, the name that kept coming up was Dr Ludwig Guttman, the founder of the Paralympics. There is no denying his part in the disability rights movement but he is a non-disabled man. Where are the articles and the history about the disabled people who protested on the frontline? Where are their stories?

I've often clashed with older disability activists who believe younger people like myself don't recognise the past as much as we should, and while I agree that we don't have as much knowledge as we'd like, I also want to demonstrate how hard it is to come by that knowledge. We should be telling the stories of disabled people from yesterday, today and tomorrow. Disabled people are not a monolith and our stories and history deserve to be told, so that the next generation of disabled activists are not left in the dark, as we have been.

For me, the upcoming disability history month is as much a chance for me to educate myself as it is for non-disabled people to educate themselves – and I'm no longer ashamed to admit that.

6 November 2020

'My son has learning disabilities. I live in fear I'll get Covid and won't be able to look after him'

For 57 years, Dame Philippa Russell has cared for her son, Simon. Now Phillipa worries about becoming unable to care for him.

By Radhika Sanghani

Philippa, 82

I've been caring for Simon since I was 25. He has learning disabilities and brain damage.

It's not so much a matter of him having to be watched every minute of the day – he's mobile, and perfectly capable of getting dressed, and he can put a simple meal in a microwave – but he has to be supported and helped. So he has to be told when to wash his clothes, he needs some meals cooked for him, and if he's going out, somebody always has to go with him.

He lives around the corner from our family home in Chichester, in a small house that my late husband Alan and I bought him, and his support worker visits a few times a week, plus I see him every evening. At weekends he's with me all the time. I'm constantly worrying something will happen to me – and since the Covid-19 crisis began, I've lived in fear that I'll get sick and won't be able to take care of Simon. He was a baby when it became obvious he wasn't developing properly. At the time we were living in central Africa as Alan was on a Foreign Office posting. When we returned to the UK, Simon was diagnosed with hydrocephalus [a build-up of fluid in the brain]. He had to have neurosurgery, and his development was slow. We were devastated – not because we cared about Simon any less, but because we worried about the life he would lead and his future. We knew there was huge prejudice against people with learning disabilities. We were given the option to put him in a long-term hospital, but we said no.

We were lucky to have Professor Ronnie MacKeith, a magnificent child-health specialist, as his doctor, and he told me: 'Your son can have a life. He will have a life. But you've got to be his advocate and help him have the life you want him to lead.'

It was very good advice, though it was challenging. I was working full-time [campaigning for Mencap and later as a director of the Council for Disabled Children], my husband was head of a division in Brussels and commuted there from our house in Highgate, and we also had two younger children, Christopher and Emma. They're now both in their 50s and I recently asked them if it had affected their lives that Simon took such a huge amount of my time. They said,

'Yes, but it should have done because Simon needed you more.' It's the age-old thing of caring: balancing everyone's care needs.

From the age of eight Simon was a weekly boarder at a residential school in Surrey where he was very, very happy. I was also lucky and had a succession of wonderful au pairs, as I accepted that if I wanted to work, there had to be support. It was hard and like many women who work and have children, you wonder afterwards if you got the balance right. But you do your best.

The hardest times have been in recent years. Alan died from cancer just before the first lockdown, and I had cared for him along with Simon, who didn't understand what was going on, all while wishing I could support Emma, who has two children, and be there for Christopher, an IT consultant based in London. I felt torn then. It was the worst time of my life. I'd cry on the train, hidden behind a newspaper, and think I couldn't go on.

The pandemic has impacted us hugely, particularly Simon. Painting is a big thing in his life and he used to go to an art programme at a local gallery. Some

people call it a 'day service', but for him it was a life. That's had to shut, which has been a disaster for him. So has the local church, where he used to go for coffees, and his favourite café where everyone knew him. With Covid-19, you lose those relationships you've built up, and for someone like Simon, it's a disaster. The loss of face-to-face contact is huge for him. I'm well connected and use Zoom, but he can't manage a video or telephone call.

It makes me very sad and worried. We'd all worked very hard to help Simon become a member of his local community and feel valued – then suddenly everyone was in masks, afraid, and the world shut down around him. It has made me very protective, but also worried about what society might look like afterwards and how Simon will be able to integrate.

We had to cancel his 57th-birthday celebrations because of lockdown – his brother and sister were planning to visit, as well as his support workers past and present – and he feels Covid has stolen his birthday. Birthdays matter to all of us, but for people like Simon, they're even more important. Seeing him so sad made me feel very helpless.

My biggest dread is that Simon will get the coronavirus – he's very vulnerable if he does – and I can't imagine how he would cope in hospital if I'm not allowed to be there with him.

I also struggle to think what Christmas will be like. Simon's has a particular ritual – he likes to go shopping in Portsmouth and attend particular carol services. I don't think things will open up in the same way. My instinct is it will be a digitally connected Christmas, but a very lonely one. My heart sinks when I think about it.

Like most parents, I worry terribly about what the future will bring. But that worry is multiplied because of how much Simon depends on me. I'm constantly anxious, and not only about Covid. What if I become ill? What if I have a fall? I always wear flat shoes in case I trip over. I need a routine eye operation, but I can't imagine how I'll have it because how can I rest for two weeks afterwards?

I'm in my 80s; I hope I'll continue well into my 90s like a lot of my relatives have, but I can't guarantee it. Simon is one of the first generation of people with learning disabilities who will probably outlive their parents. We've set up a family trust that will release money, and I'm sure my two other children will support him, but I want them to be his brother and sister not his carers, as when you're a carer it really does change your relationship.

When Alan was alive, there were always three people in the marriage – Simon was one of them. We weren't able to do the things that other couples do, and never had a holiday on our own after he was born. I don't regret it – it would have felt wrong to go away without Simon – but I always advise younger carers to make sure they still recognise they're their own person, as well.

Caring for someone is very lonely, but I feel lucky to have found a remarkable community of fellow carers over the years, and that's something the charity Carers UK has helped with. I've made connections I never would have made if I hadn't been in this position, and during lockdown, which could easily have been such a lonely time with both Simon and I shielding, I stayed in touch with them via Zoom calls. I do worry that there are a lot of older carers behind closed doors who don't have access to resources like that.

I think ageism is rife in our society, and it's hard for many older carers because they can suddenly be put in that role and it's a very strange world. It's different for me because I've been doing it my whole life. And I know I'm just as capable of caring for Simon in my 80s as I was in my 40s.

Simon, 57

I love having mum around the corner and I feel safe because she's there. She cooks me lots of dinners, things like roast chicken, casseroles and pasta. I also have a support worker, but things are difficult for him too, with Covid-19, so he has to be very careful and we can't do all the things we usually do.

The pandemic has changed things a lot. It's made me feel very lonely, as I can't go to my art classes, which was my favourite day activity. I used to love going to the café and the church too, because I see people there. There are two very friendly priests. But everything is closed now.

It's going on and on. I feel shut out of things and I wish I could have my old life back. Before, Mum and I used to go to the theatre, the cinema and cafés. We'd go and see my brother and sister and my nephews, but we can't now.

I went for a meal with my current and old support workers, just before lockdown. And one weekend, my sister brought me a vegan chocolate cake she'd baked for my birthday. It was nice, but I was very disappointed because I like it when everyone comes together and having everybody around the table, but this year they just couldn't.

I used to work at a garden centre, and for a while at B&Q, but those jobs went and since then I've been doing art. I like to paint landscapes and buildings – I've had some pictures accepted for exhibitions. I used to do this outside with my support worker, but that's impossible now [because of Covid], so I just use my imagination.

When Covid-19 goes away, I can't wait to go back to my art classes and see my friends. I hope Christmas will be like normal. It's my favourite time. I love decorating the house and watching the lighting of the Christmas tree in Chichester.

If Christmas was off this year, I'd be very sad. I'd want to write to the Prime Minister: I'd say to him, 'Boris, please make Christmas happen because it really matters.

12 December 2020

I felt powerless in the pandemic trying to get food and essentials while shielding

By Melanie Duddridge

I'm Melanie, and I'm 48. I'm from Florida originally, but I moved to Wales 11 years ago to join my husband.

I myself am disabled and I can't work. I have pretty severe Crohn's disease, an autoimmune disease throughout the entire digestive system. The main symptoms I get are severe pain and upset stomach, and I've had quite a few major bowel surgeries.

I also have fibromyalgia, which came along after I had cancer in 2014. Fibromyalgia causes me pain throughout my entire body and limits my mobility, and because it's chronic, it fluctuates. Some days, I can do more than others.

As a result of my fibromyalgia and Crohn's, I also have chronic fatigue.

It's a challenge to be a disabled mother. My daughter is under assessment for potential autism, but we're still waiting on a final assessment and it has been delayed by years because of coronavirus. All these factors mean I rely on my husband quite a bit, he's basically my carer.

Before the pandemic

Before the pandemic, I'd shop at Tesco. I liked their rewards programme, their customer service is good, and we'd take advantage of their Click and Collect.

As a disabled person, I feel confident with the bigger stores - that there's going to be an obvious bathroom that's clean, and there's going to be a wheelchair if I need it. The bathrooms are very well marked and easy to find, usually at the front of the store, and that can be enough just to get me in at times.

The fact Tesco have electric wheelchairs has helped me many times. For example, after surgery, or if I'm in too much pain but I need to go to the shops.

The start of the pandemic and accessibility barriers

At the start of the pandemic, I couldn't get a delivery. Supermarkets weren't answering the phone, so I couldn't get through to find out store layouts and accessibility information. For me, these aren't just preferences, they're necessities.

As lockdowns continued, I started to hear how people with hidden disabilities were really struggling to be recognised in stores. Naturally, I had a lot of concerns about the one-way systems supermarkets had put into place. Looking at me, you wouldn't know I might need to jump the one-way system, or that I'd need to start at the toilet, not end at it.

How long would I have to be standing? Are there any tight areas where I'd get too close to people? If I needed the toilet, did I have to go around, up and down every aisle and around the store to get there?

Without knowing exactly where these things were positioned, it was anxiety-inducing.

Because my husband is my carer, I don't really go anywhere without him. And because I wasn't allowed into stores with him, it just wasn't happening.

There was no way for me to shop, so initially, I was relying on a local volunteer network to support me with getting food.

Online accessibility during the pandemic

I was getting lots of emails with different information from Tesco, but I was having trouble getting delivery slots with them. They were just sold out of everything, So I registered with Morrisons, Asda, Waitrose, Sainsbury's, I was checking everywhere. There was a lot of anxiety and time put into finding those slots, to try to meet my family's needs.

There was the frustration of navigating different supermarket websites and finding the products you needed in a different format. I just felt like sometimes like I didn't have the resources to do all that, to keep checking and learning the new website, and coming up empty.

If I had to go without food, I would. But the thought of not having food for my daughter was devastating. And there was nothing I could do but sit on my computer and sign up for all those supermarkets.

Everything felt completely out of my control. I had no power. No-one was meeting my needs. I couldn't go to the shops because they weren't accessible for me, and because I was clinically extremely vulnerable and shielding.

There was a lot of desperation. It was like my purpose as a mother was under question. They were really dark times.

Supermarket which met my needs

After finally being put on the priority list, I found that a lot those priority slots were more expensive and there was an 8-hour delivery window, which wasn't practical.

It took the pandemic to force me to look at other supermarkets. And one that stood out for me was Asda - they were actually there for me, to meet my needs.

I didn't have to notify them I was on the shielding list. All of a sudden, the priority slots just appeared, and there was hope. They had lots of slots late at night, and extra drivers with deliveries for £1, which made a real difference. Because of all these factors, I feel a connection with them. I feel like they've heard me, and they care.

I'm so thankful that we were eventually able to find a solution that worked for us. But it should never have been that difficult to be able to get food and essentials in the middle of a pandemic. We really did feel forgotten.

The in-store experience of disabled people needed to improve before the pandemic struck.

As well as considering keeping some coronavirus safety measures in place, Scope believes retailers need to provide disability awareness training for all in-store supermarket staff. They should also make a public commitment to their disabled customers, and have a clear public-facing strategy to detail how they will be more inclusive towards disabled customers.

15 July 2021

Disabled people experience more disability hate crime in public than online

A survey conducted by Disability Horizons and disability charity Leonard Cheshire has found disabled people have experienced more disability hate crime in public than online in the past three years.

More than half (53%) of the 196 people* who responded to our survey said they have experienced hate crime in a public place in the past three years, with 32 people seeing them happening during the coronavirus pandemic. In contrast, only 43 people have been a victim of hate crime online, with 19 people reporting them occurring during the Covid-19 crisis.

Disability hate crime in public

Of those who have been subject to disability hate crime in public in the last three years (105), 49% have experienced it between two to five times.

47% said they've experienced verbal abuse aimed directly at them, such as shouting and name-calling.

When asked about reporting incidences of disability hate crime in a public place:

♦ 56% didn't report it

♦ 21% reported to staff at the public place

♦ 19% (20 people) reported to the police.

Inappropriate exposure at a wheelchair user

A wheelchair user was verbally victimised by teenagers at a bus station, which left them mentally traumatised:

"I went past some youths, in my powerchair, at a bus station. Suddenly one of them came running from behind me, stopped suddenly in front of me, dropped his trousers and his pants to expose himself."

He (and his friends) laughed and he said something about me needing some of this while pointing to his genitals. He then pulled his clothing back up and ran off.

"Although I wasn't hurt, a few minutes later I started crying uncontrollably and several people came to comfort me. I couldn't get the incident out of my mind for months.

"At the time I hadn't even given him a withering look, and I was so disappointed with myself for not taking any action at the time."

Blue Badge holders judging others

Disability hate crime doesn't just come from non-disabled people, but also other disabled people:

"I've been verbally attacked and my car banged on before I could even put my Blue Badge inside my window.

This happens frequently and is often by other disabled Blue Badge holders. Because I'm younger than some badge holders, I get targeted by older people."

Lazy scrounger comments

One respondent witnessed offensive comments about disabled people from someone she knew while out at a bar:

"Once, the landlady and my former employer ranted on about two disabled friends of mine – one who has schizophrenia and was born with just one hand, and the other who has brain damage after a horrific car accident.

"She said that they were lazy scroungers of the state for not working, all just three feet away from me.

"I also can't work because of my MS and mental health problems. It shocked me so much that I haven't left my flat since that incident three years ago."

9 of the 105 people who have been victims of disability hate crime have experienced physical abuse, such as hitting and spitting.

Physical abuse on a pelican crossing

A woman who uses two crutches was physically and mentally traumatised after being attacked on a main road:

"My husband had taken me to the hairdressers in the city centre. Coming out, I had to cross the main road to return to the car park where my husband was waiting.

"The pelican crossing was very busy, and there were buses and cars revving their engines. I started to make my way across the road when two young men started loudly making comments.

"I tried to ignore it and kept my head down, but one said to the other, "The fat, ugly bitch on crutches is yours" and then pushed him hard into me.

"I lost my balance and fell to the ground, my sticks out of my reach and the lights changed.

"They ran off and I panicked and grabbed about retrieving my sticks, other people just walking around me.

"I shuffled on my bottom to the pavement and pulled myself up on the post of the pelican crossing. I was grazed and bleeding but worse still, I was completely traumatised."

Disability hate crime in public during Covid-19

Only 32 people we surveyed said they've experienced disability hate crime in public during the coronavirus pandemic, with 14 saying it was specifically because of Covid-19.

The majority of these incidents were related to the face mask exemptions.

Verbal abuse for removing face mask to lip read

Karolina Pakenaite, who has Usher syndrome, and her 16-year-old sister, Saule, were confronted by another passenger on a train after Saule removed her face mask so that her deaf-blind sister could lip read. Karolina told us:

"I am the girl on the news who got attacked on the train because I needed to enable my sister to lip read."

Stopped by shop workers for not wearing a face mask

A customer with a health condition that causes breathing difficulties was stopped by shop staff for not wearing a face mask:

"I've been pointed at, talked about and even stopped by shop workers for not wearing a mask. I have acute asthma, bronchitis and allergies, including cardiopulmonary urticaria."

Disabled person told to shield accused of being lazy

As well as being criticised for not wearing face masks, disabled people shielding have been accused of being lazy:

"I was told I should go out and get my own groceries instead of shielding even though I was told to do so. I was called a lazy, scrounging foreigner and that there was nothing wrong with me."

You can read our full article about the abuse disabled people have been getting about the face mask exemptions, including from other disabled people.

Disability hate crime online

Out of the 43 people who have been victims of disability hate crime online, 22 have experienced it more than once but less than five times.

22 people have had a disability hate crime committed by a named stranger online.

Our stats also show that Facebook is the most common place for disability hate crime online, with 30 respondents saying they've been victimised on the social media platform and/or the messenger service.

Facebook user told they'd be better off dead

A member of a Facebook page was sharing the difficulties of their health condition when another user commented that they'd be better off dead:

"On Facebook a person was saying that what I was going through was all in my head and that if it was that bad I would have been better off not here as I don't want to get better.

The person had been having a go at others on the page, so admin stepped in shut the post down and removed the person making the comments."

Grandparent accused of lying about their disability

A Facebook user accused a grandparent of lying about their disability because they believed disabled people can't travel abroad:

"I am proud to be a spoonie; a disabled person with a fluctuating condition" – this is on my Facebook page, in my open details and in my photos.

Someone I have never met took it upon themselves to tell me that I was lying about being disabled as I had shared my experiences of having taken a trip to Canada to visit my grandchildren.

They said that if I was really disabled It would be impossible for me to drive or to fly as disabled people are incapable of doing those activities.

I politely pointed out that lots of disabled people drive and travel all over the world, including mountain climbing. I cannot write his response to that, which was removed by Facebook within the hour, as it is just too disgusting for words."

Blogger victim of hateful slurs online

A disability blogger was subject to offensive comments and hate speech on their online platform:

"I run a blog that tries to help young disabled people and someone started a hate campaign calling me 'crippled bitch' and 'retarded'".

It was also claimed that I should have been drowned at birth, or "killed for the betterment of society". It lasted for a while as it took the site time to see that it as a hate crime despite the use of slurs and specific wording."

Disability hate crime online during Covid-19

19 respondents have experienced hate crime online during the coronavirus pandemic, with 13 of them saying it happened because of Covid-19.

Saying thank you was met by hateful comments

A disabled person who received food parcels over lockdown simply wanted to say thank you but got a backlash of abuse online:

"It was on Facebook, actually a government page. I'd been receiving the Provisions Box during the lockdown and I just wanted to say thank you to the government and the British Taxpayers for this privilege.

After I'd posted a message of thanks I began receiving so many negative messages accusing me of being a lazy taker.

I posted a couple of lines about my personal disabilities and received the most hateful, nasty, upsetting messages, such as "I should be dead if I'm so disabled" and "people like me shouldn't get free stuff". They even accused me of being a "druggie" and worse.

I found it to be very hateful and extremely upsetting. I'm simply a retired NHS amputee who wanted to say thank you."

Criticism over face mask exemptions

Two respondents told us how they've received online abuse for being exempt from wearing a face mask.

One person said: "Every single day I'm told that if I can't wear a mask I should stay indoors, that Covid should have got me, that only those with underlying conditions die as if that justifies our higher death rates."

Another person has found a creative way to tackle hateful comments online: "I've been trolled on Facebook groups, mainly due me being exempt from wearing a face mask.

Other people think people like me who are "unmasked" should not be allowed to do what everyone else can do now. I have set up a self-help group in response rather than complain."

Reports of violent disability hate crime continue to rise

In addition to this survey with Disability Horizons, Leonard Cheshire also conducted research with fellow charity United Response.

They found that reports of disability hate crime are up 12% across 36 regions in England and Wales in 2019/20 but only 1.6% of cases resulted in police charging the perpetrators.

*The survey was conducted in August and September 2020. We surveyed 196 UK residents who consider themselves to be disabled or have a long-term health condition.

This data is not representative of a wider population, nor is it weighted.

28 October 2020

Disability discrimination

What is disability discrimination?

Disability discrimination is when you are treated less well or put at a disadvantage for a reason that relates to your disability in one of the situations covered by the Equality Act.

The treatment could be a one-off action, the application of a rule or policy or the existence of physical or communication barriers which make accessing something difficult or impossible.

The discrimination does not have to be intentional to be unlawful.

What the Equality Act says about disability discrimination

The Equality Act 2010 says that you must not be discriminated against because:

♦   you have a disability

♦   someone thinks you have a disability (this is known as discrimination by perception)

♦   you are connected to someone with a disability (this is known as discrimination by association)

It is not unlawful discrimination to treat a disabled person more favourably than a nondisabled person.

What is classed as a disability?

In the Equality Act a disability means a physical or a mental condition which has a substantial and long-term impact on your ability to do normal day to day activities.

You are covered by the Equality Act if you have a progressive condition like HIV, cancer or multiple sclerosis, even if you are currently able to carry out normal day to day activities. You are protected as soon as you are diagnosed with a progressive condition.

You are also covered by the Equality Act if you had a disability in the past. For example, if you had a mental health condition in the past which lasted for over 12 months, but you have now recovered, you are still protected from discrimination because of that disability.

Different types of disability discrimination

There are six main types of disability discrimination:

♦   direct discrimination

♦   indirect discrimination

♦   failure to make reasonable adjustments

♦   discrimination arising from disability

- harassment
- victimisation

Direct discrimination

This happens when someone treats you worse than another person in a similar situation because of disability. For example:

during an interview, a job applicant tells the potential employer that he has multiple sclerosis. The employer decides not to appoint him even though he's the best candidate they have interviewed, because they assume he will need a lot of time off sick

Indirect discrimination

Indirect discrimination happens when an organisation has a particular policy or way of working that has a worse impact on disabled people compared to people who are not disabled.

Indirect disability discrimination is unlawful unless the organisation or employer is able to show that there is a good reason for the policy and it is proportionate.

This is known as objective justification. For example:

a job advert states that all applicants must have a driving licence. This puts some disabled people at a disadvantage because they may not have a licence because, for example, they have epilepsy. If the advert is for a bus driver job, the requirement will

be justified. If it is for a teacher to work across two schools, it will be more difficult to justify

Failure to make reasonable adjustments

Under the Equality Act employers and organisations have a responsibility to make sure that disabled people can access jobs, education and services as easily as non-disabled people. This is known as the 'duty to make reasonable adjustments'.

Disabled people can experience discrimination if the employer or organisation doesn't make a reasonable adjustment. This is known as a 'failure to make reasonable adjustments'. For example:

an employee with mobility impairment needs a parking space close to the office. However, her employer only gives parking spaces to senior managers and refuses to give her a designated parking space

What is reasonable depends on a number of factors, including the resources available to the organisation making the adjustment. If an organisation already has a number of parking spaces it would be reasonable for it to designate one close to the entrance for the employee.

Discrimination arising from disability

The Equality Act also protects people from discrimination arising from disability.

This protects you from being treated badly because of something connected to your disability, such as having an assistance dog or needing time off for medical appointments. This does not apply unless the person who discriminated against you knew you had a disability or ought to have known. For example:

- a private nursery refuses to give a place to a little boy because he is not toilet trained. His parents have told them that he isn't toilet trained because he has Hirschsprung's Disease, but they still refuse to give him a place. This is discrimination arising from the little boy's disability

- an employee with cancer is prevented from receiving a bonus because of time she has taken off to receive treatment

Discrimination arising from disability is unlawful unless the organisation or employer is able to show that there is a good reason for the treatment and it is proportionate. This is known as objective justification. For example:

an employee whose eyesight has seriously deteriorated cannot do as much work as his non-disabled colleagues. If his employer sought to dismiss him, after ruling out the possibility of redeployment, the employer

would need to show that this was for good reason and was proportionate

Harassment

Harassment occurs when someone treats you in a way that makes you feel humiliated, offended or degraded. For example:

a disabled woman is regularly sworn at and called names by colleagues at work because of her disability

Harassment can never be justified. However, if an organisation or employer can show it did everything it could to prevent people who work for it from behaving like that, you will not be able to make a claim for harassment against it, although you could make a claim against the harasser.

Victimisation

This is when you are treated badly because you have made a complaint of discrimination under the Equality Act. It can also occur if you are supporting someone who has made a complaint of discrimination. For example:

- an employee has made a complaint of disability discrimination. The employer threatens to sack them unless they withdraw the complaint

- an employer threatens to sack a member of staff because he thinks she intends to support a colleague's disability discrimination claim

Circumstances when being treated differently due to disability is lawful

Non-disabled people

It is always lawful to treat a disabled person more favourably than a non-disabled person.

Other disabled people

Treating a disabled person with a particular disability more favourably than other disabled people may be lawful in some circumstances. For example:

- where having a particular disability is essential for the job (this is called an occupational requirement). For example, an organisation supporting deaf people might require that an employee whose role is providing counselling to British Sign Language users is a deaf BSL user

- where an organisation is taking positive action to encourage or develop people with a particular disability. For example, an employer is aware that people with learning disabilities have a particularly high rate of unemployment, so sets up a mentoring and job-shadowing programme for people with learning disabilities to help them prepare to apply for jobs

Occupational requirement and positive action are clarified in our statutory code of practice on employment.

What else does the Equality Act protect against?

Being asked health questions designed to screen out disabled job applicants.

The Equality Act says that employers cannot ask job applicants about their health or disability until they have been offered a job, except in specific circumstances where the information is necessary for the application process or a requirement of the job. For example:

a job applicant fills in an application form which asks people to state whether they are taking any medication. Unless there is a good reason why the employer needs to know this information, then the question should not be asked

This text is adapted from the Equality Advisory and Support Service (EASS): www.equalityadvisoryservice.com

Last updated: 18 Feb 2020

Are we facing a disability discrimination crisis?

By ShoutOutUK

Over the last few years it seems that much of the progress made in helping disabled people feel more welcomed and more equal in society has been reversed. We hear more stories of individuals discriminated against by businesses, government, transport staff, and members of the public — although everybody is always very apologetic afterwards. While we have shows such as The Last Leg, and travel presenters such as Ade Adepitan, showing the nation that being disabled no longer means you have to be sidelined and ignored, many people still struggle day to day. So what went wrong, and can it be fixed?

Rail travellers discriminated

To highlight the problems, let's look at a few of the worst cases of discrimination we've seen over the last year. In many of these cases disabled people have been made to feel unwelcome and insulted in public places.

In July 2018, Tanyalee Davis, a disabled comedian, was 'harassed and humiliated' when she used a disabled space for her mobility scooter. The train guard threatened to report her to the police. The reason for the conflict was that a young mother wished to park her pram in the space reserved for the disabled. It is hard to believe that in today's Britain a member of the public would complain that a disabled passenger was using the disabled space for their mobility scooter; and worse, that rail staff would threaten to call the police to remove the disabled person. Maybe we should be grateful that she was not dragged off the train.

Great Western Railway (GWR) said they were 'collectively horrified', and were very sorry. But, that was not the end of her problems, as only a few days later, station staff told the train guard she had been helped off a train, when in fact she had been left waiting by the doors. She missed her stop. An LNER spokesperson said:

'We are very sorry for the unacceptable experience Ms Davis had whilst travelling with us'.

Finally, in October an autistic boy was mocked by GWR staff at Paddington Station. His mother asked if it would be possible to catch an earlier train as they were two hours early and her son was finding the intensity of the station challenging. The result was jeering staff accusing her of fraud. A GWR spokesperson said:

'We are sorry to learn of Sarah's experience … '

If you think that these might be isolated cases, you are wrong. The Metro reported last year that rail staff have been told not to help disabled people board trains if it is likely to cause a delay. Disabled people are officially second-class citizens when it comes to travel.

Discrimination in the air

In August 2018, Jack Johnson a 10-year-old disabled boy, was asked to prove that he was disabled before he was allowed to use a mobility scooter. It took two hours before Jet2 staff allowed him to board a flight. Jet2 said sorry.

In September more discrimination against the disabled was carried out by Ryanair staff. A grandmother and her disabled son were forced to leave a Ryanair flight because staff couldn't work out how to fold his electric wheelchair. They were offered a flight the following day, but again staff struggled with his folding powerchair, and the captain apologised … to the rest of the passengers for delay caused by 'the lady with the wheelchair'. OmniServ and Liverpool Airport all said sorry afterwards.

Disabled are being left behind

Being left behind is a common problem for the disabled. You'd think staff would be aware of the risk of generating more bad publicity, but the BBC's security correspondent, Frank Gardner, was left on an empty plane at Heathow Airport twice in one year. On one occasion he was stuck for two hours after staff lost his wheelchair — somebody took the wheelchair to the terminal, not realising it's owner might need it. Guess what? The airport apologised.

Shoppers discriminated

You don't have to go far to experience discrimination if you are disabled. Asda staff decided in December 2018 to ban mobility scooters from their cafe. Staff suggested that one customer should, 'return the scooter and walk back to the café'. Very helpful.

But more shocking than this, in November a disabled customer in Pret A Manger dared to use the disabled toilets. On exiting the toilet, Kirsty Llloyd was shouted at by Pret staff, which was both embarrassing and shocking for her. The reason for the attack — the staff didn't understand, or even ask, about her disability. Pret said 'we're really sorry about the treatment Kirsty received at our shop'.

Councils cutting free transport for disabled

It is not just trains and planes that discriminate though. Thanks to austerity, many councils are cutting free school bus services for disabled children to specialist schools.

In Coventry, 16-year-old Sara Grove had been given free school transport from the age of three, but at sixteen this service was cancelled and her mum was asked to pay £600.

Specialist schools are usually many miles from the homes of the children that attend them. The charity Contact has seen similar cases in Leicestershire, West Sussex, North Yorkshire, Leeds, Hampshire, Oxfordshire and Suffolk.

And it is not just school children who are having their transport cut. In Nottingham, free bus and tram travel for disabled people has been cut. Nottingham East MP Chris Leslie described the situation as:

'a step backwards for equal opportunities'.

Now is the time — stop saying sorry!

It seems that everybody is always very sorry for being so rude and discriminatory towards disabled people. So why does it carry on? We see both government policy and business procedures making it harder for disabled people to travel on planes, trains and buses.

Disabled people are also reporting increased discrimination from other members of the public. Whenever the government, organisations and businesses publicly discriminate, it sends out a clear message — it's open season on the disabled, everybody can have a go.

In January this year Scope launched a new campaign, Now Is The Time, to raise awareness of discrimination against the disabled. Scope's research has revealed that '87% of parents have felt judged by members of the public, 41% of them were offered no emotional support'. Scope is asking the government to appoint a Minister for Disabled Children and Families, and for more funding to be made available to families to provide emotional support for the whole family.

Support movements such as Scope and Disability Awareness in Action, and work with organisations in schools and colleges. The only way to overcome discrimination is to fight it head on. Raise awareness, shout out, and be the generation that brings about positive change.

13 March 2019

Rhetoric versus reality: how Britain treats people with disabilities

Alain Catzeflis explores the impact of Conservative ideology, austerity and the Coronavirus on people who the Government claims it wants to protect and support.

By Alain Catzefelis

The number of people with a learning disability who died this year in England and Wales (not in hospitals or the community but in care settings alone) was up by 134% compared to the same period in 2019. This is a preliminary and conservative estimate.

The comparable figure for the number of excess deaths in the general population is around 35%. Therefore someone with a learning disability is, shockingly, nearly four times more likely to have died with COVID-19.

The Care Quality Commission – in a statement that came as close to slamming the Government as it dare – said: "We already know that people with a learning disability are at an increased risk of respiratory illnesses, meaning that access to testing could be key to reducing infection and saving lives."

Attitudes to disability, like attitudes to race, have not evolved in a smooth upward curve.

For the most part, it has been a case of two steps forward and one step back. Since 2010, and the politics of austerity, the direction of travel has been mostly backwards.

For centuries, those with disabilities were deemed untouchable, locked up in asylums – prisons dressed up as charity – paraded as 'freaks' or subjected to eugenics or euthanasia.

Even the wise were prejudiced. Aristotle said the deaf were "incapable of reason".

Charles Dickens, well-meaning as he was, created characters with disabilities such as Tiny Tim in A Christmas Carol – who were helpless, but deserving – and weaponised pity. The late Australian comedian Stella Young called this 'inspirational porn".

On paper, Britain has some of the most progressive disability legislation – laws brimming with good intentions: the landmark Disability Discrimination Act (1995), the Mental Capacity Act (2005), the Equality Act (2010), and the Care Act (2014).

We like to think that Britain is a fair country and looking after the most vulnerable, even when times are tough, is an anthem governments repeat. But the reality is very different.

After years of hard-won progress and a decade of austerity, those with disabilities now find themselves – again – in the fight of their lives. They remain the object of injustice, prejudice, hate crimes, economic policies that target them unfairly and a welfare system that is deeply flawed and sometimes fatally punitive.

People with a disability are much more likely to be living in poverty. They face extra costs to do the same things that people without a disability do, described by the Social Metrics Commission as the "inescapable cost of disability". A disabled family with the same income as a non-disabled family is inevitably worse-off.

In 2017, the Equality and Human Rights Commission in its report 'Being Disabled in Britain: A journey Less Equal' stated: "At face value we have travelled far… But the road to disability equality is littered with missed opportunities and failure. It is a badge of shame on our society and successive governments."

The report found that, as a result of austerity, some disabled people were set to lose £11,000 on average by 2021-2022 – "driving many families to breaking point".

The rot set in following the 2008 financial crisis. A recession, caused by bankers who were subsequently bailed out by the taxpayer, led to a targeted austerity that punished the poorest and most vulnerable by slashing and then freezing public sector spending.

This assault on the living standards of those with disabilities reflected a pincer movement: brutal cuts to services by central Government and local authorities on one side and a series of welfare 'reforms' on the other that have made it much harder to cope in tough times and driven many into unaffordable debt, food banks, ill-health and sometimes suicide.

Local councils have lost nearly £16 billion in core funding since 2010, equating to 60%. By 2025, the Local Government Association estimates that adult social care in England and Wales alone faces a deficit of £3.5 billion.

Support services for people with disabilities have been cut to the bone. Welfare budgets have been hollowed out; measures intended to create a level playing field have been eviscerated; recourse to law for wrongful decisions has been choked off by swingeing legal aid cuts. Many individuals with disabilities, like victims of racial prejudice, are voiceless because they can't afford a lawyer. They can only challenge life-changing injustice by relying on the charity of civic-minded lawyers.

The other side of the pincer movement has been the drive to 'streamline' welfare, ostensibly to make it more efficient. In reality, it is a core part of the Conservative strategy to shrink the state by cutting back on public spending.

Two key changes to the benefit system have had a huge impact on the lives of people with disabilities: the introduction of Personal Independence Payments (PIP) replacing Disability Living Allowance (DLA), and the new Universal Credit – the brainchild of former Conservative Party leader Iain Duncan Smith.

The phased roll-out of the new PIP scheme in 2013 meant that all people with disabilities or a chronic illness, without exception, had to be re-assessed for a disability benefit. This complex and sensitive process was outsourced, with hardly any oversight, to private companies employing health 'professionals' – some with barely a month's training.

The monthly Universal Credit payment amalgamates six benefits into one, which the Government claimed is easier for job-seekers and families with low earnings to claim benefits. For some it is, but for many it is not. Most of those claiming it live week-to-week, some day-to-day. A bank transfer that is a month or more away for many means asking for an emergency loan, yet more paperwork, or a visit to the pawn shop.

Alongside this, sits the Work Capability Assessment – a densely packed 25-page form followed, in some cases, by a face-to-face interrogation. Whether the claimant receives an assessment that is sensible and fair, or whether they feel they have been subjected – as many do – to a process that is intrusive, humiliating and – in the case of people whose condition will never change – pointless, is pot luck. It is a tick-box exercise in which officials with no medical training make life-changing and sometimes life-ending decisions. One claimant with Down's Syndrome was asked: "How did you catch it?"

Claimants can be sanctioned for missing an appointment or not meeting an arbitrary target for job applications between reviews. Money is docked, sometimes stopped altogether, catapulting families into crisis. Those with disabilities have gone from being untouchable to being unaffordable, as Dr Frances Ryan argues in her book Crippled.

The failure of these reforms is stark and self-evident.

By 2020, the Government will have paid out nearly £1 billion to people with disabilities wrongfully withheld support. An astonishing 60-70% of those with disabilities either declared fit for work or who challenged their PIP assessments won their case on appeal.

By 2019, the Department for Work and Pensions and the Ministry of Justice had spent a staggering £200 million – either on direct staff or legal costs defending decisions, most of which were overturned on appeal.

In November 2017, Sir Ernest Ryder, Senior President of Tribunals, said that the evidence provided by the Government in defence of its decisions was "so poor it would be wholly inadmissible" in any other court. More than 60% of cases, he added, presented to tribunals were "no-brainers. They just shouldn't be there".

The decision to heap austerity cuts on the vulnerable not only went against the principle of fairness, it also failed to achieve its intended fiscal aim to reduce the budget deficit. It has been a failure on both fronts – tacitly acknowledged by the Government, under enormous pressure, by exempting people with the most serious disabilities and chronic illnesses from reassessment.

Perhaps the most sinister aspect of this assault on people with disabilities is the narrative that accompanies it: the 'bogus disabled' pumped out by successive Cabinet ministers; mood music that divides people into 'strivers' and 'scroungers'; rhetoric of a 'something for nothing culture'.

This is a tragedy. With the right support people with disabilities can lead rich and fulfilling lives – as documented in Saba Salman's excellent book Made Possible.

Britain has a long way to go with this. A start would be to recognise that disability is a big and complex subject that cannot continue to play second fiddle to health and work. We need a Secretary of State for People with Disabilities with Cabinet status (as exists in France, Finland and Portugal) to redefine the narrative and find ways of giving people with disabilities the dignity and respect they deserve.

16 June 2020

'People have outdated views about disabled performers': Line of Duty's Tommy Jessop on acting with Down's Syndrome

He's been called 'phenomenal' by Mark Rylance, acted alongside Vicky McClure, played Hamlet, and taken part in critically acclaimed shorts, but Tommy Jessop believes there's still much progress to be made in how the film industry treats disabled actors.

By Andy Morris

Tommy Jessop was 22 when he first saw a character with Down's syndrome on screen. "It was … me!" he says with a grin, sitting in his family's living room. In the BBC TV drama Coming Down the Mountain in 2007, Jessop played a disabled teenager despised by his older brother. It captured Jessop's ability to fully realise his characters on screen.

"Making viewers feel emotions is my passion in life," says Jessop.

In person, the 36-year-old is animated company. There are many things Jessop thinks are either "brilliant" or "wicked", including but not limited to: receiving an honorary doctorate in arts from the University of Winchester, his "top secret" new acting project, being a volunteer usher at the Theatre Royal, Callum Wilson and Allan Saint-Maximin from Newcastle United, Bradley Walsh's The Chase, and presenting an award at the 2021 Bafta ceremony. His recent passion project is cooking, where he shares the results on Twitter with his nearly 30,000 followers. ("I've made flapjacks and cakes, shepherd's pie and fish pie," he says.)

Jessop has made a career out of overcoming obstacles. Growing up in Hampshire, he developed a taste for the limelight appearing in junior school plays. "I enjoyed being the centre of attention," he says. His mother, Jane, believed it might just be a phase but Jessop kept getting cast. After he left school, Jane founded Blue Apple Theatre, a group dedicated to assisting actors with learning disabilities in taking their next steps on stage.

Her son, never ducking a challenge, took the lead in the Blue Apple Theatre's touring production of Hamlet. "That was one of my personal highlights in my career," he remembers. "I learned how to sword fight and to do the famous speech, to be or not to be." No less than former Royal Shakespeare

Company legend Mark Rylance told Jessop his performance was "phenomenal".

Jessop was fortunate enough to be selected from hundreds of applicants for the Talent Fund for Disabled Actors – a bursary scheme organised by the BBC, Channel 4 and the Actors Centre – which helps nurture talent by running sessions for young people with top directors and industry figures. He started getting key TV roles in medical dramas such as Casualty and Holby City, building up his confidence and knowledge of the craft. Critically acclaimed dramatic roles followed in short films such as Innocence and Fighter.

Without question, however, Jessop's biggest role so far was playing Terry Boyle in Line of Duty, Jed Mercurio's hugely popular TV crime thriller. In seasons five and six, Jessop plays an unwitting victim, who, through "mate crime", is first tricked into storing a dead body in his freezer, then subsequently framed for murder. At one dramatic moment, Boyle is interrogated, then nearly drowned in a freezing lake. "Being on set was literally like being in a James Bond film," is Jessop's memory of his on-screen near death experience, comparing the temperature to "living in Antarctica" and expressing his gratitude to his "brilliant" castmate Vicky McClure for giving him a hug to warm him up.

The results were viewed by 11 million people, including, to Jessop's delight, the Queen. "I was literally speechless when I read that story," he remembers. "It was really quite overwhelming." The only drawback to appearing on a major BBC show was the ongoing health checks. "Well, you might let the Guinness World Records know: I took 21 Covid tests. It was very tough." He clearly loved every other aspect of the experience – and was certainly not fazed by the description of his character as a "local oddball" by superintendent Ted Hastings. "This is showing the world what this 'oddball' is really capable of doing: in character I've even planned a murder!" says Jessop.

Asked what advice he would give other young actors with Down's syndrome, Jessop believes you can be the agent of your own success. "Keep on dreaming and believing," he says. "One day you really will reap the rewards of your hard work." He believes passionately that disabled people need to be given chances to appear on screen, playing a wide variety of characters rather than merely timid victims or infantile objects of pity.

"Look at the type of people I've played: a murderer, a fighter, a thief, a fisherman, a football fan …"

Jessop warms to this theme. "People have outdated views about disabled performers. We have jobs and hobbies, we fall in love and out of love. Please let us show you what we can do in life and in film. If we are on screen, people will know that we can live interesting lives and have skills and talents."

Jessop believes that we can expect to see more multifaceted performances in the future.

"The biggest challenge is to persuade producers and showrunners to believe in performers like me. People making short films seem to believe in us and trust us as performers to create amazing work – people making feature films need to learn from them. Just let us play characters with the same hopes, dreams and adventures everyone else has!"

He feels there is so much more progress to be made. "I'm breaking down barriers because there was no writing for actors like me, because they didn't know we could play the roles."

He is profoundly grateful for the industry support he has received, but issues something of a challenge: "I can play any role you throw at me. Just give me a chance."

9 August 2021

Why it's time to end TV's deplorable prejudice against disabled people

Speaking at the Edinburgh Television Festival about the scandalous lack of representation and disgraceful conditions my colleagues endure means underlining systemic failures.

By Jack Thorne

I had mixed feelings on being offered the MacTaggart lecture this year. The first was surprise: had anyone ever heard me speak? I once did a Bafta speech that Piers Morgan described on Twitter as the worst in the history of the awards. The second was disbelief that I had been afforded such an honour. The third was a sense of extreme responsibility. I knew it was an opportunity to talk about disability – or the lack of disability – on TV, how television gets key discussions wrong, and how I might dare represent that cause.

The issue of representation has reared its head in the past 10 years in particular. I am not going to use the word diversity because I don't love the word. Diversity feels celebratory: "Look how diverse we are, aren't we wonderful." Representation implies a responsibility. If TV

is not representative then it fails. And when it comes to disability, the failure is really stark.

Many of these arguments are dismissed by people as woke-ism and virtue signalling. But the truth is that so much of what we do is governed by empathy, and I truly believe TV has such power in that regard.

It is clear that empathy is lacking more broadly. In her beautiful book, Crippled, the Guardian columnist Frances Ryan outlines how, since the election of David Cameron in 2010, there has been a concerted attack on disabled people in Britain. Ryan writes: "When then chancellor George Osborne promised we were "all in it together", in fact it was disabled people who were targeted to take the greatest hit, with tens of billions of pounds being pulled from everything from disability benefits to housing to social care provision. The Centre for Welfare Reform calculated in 2013 that disabled people would endure nine times the burden of cuts compared to the average citizen, with people with the most severe disabilities being hit a staggering 19 times harder … [this] was a deliberate attack on disabled people in Britain."

With the pandemic, that situation has become deadly. A new study, partly carried out by the ONS, estimated that, in England, between 24 January 2020 and 28 February 2021, 105,213 people died from causes involving Covid-19, of whom 61,000 were disabled. That's almost 60% of all deaths.

I am not claiming that TV can save lives, but it can change temperatures, and those temperature changes in turn might save lives. Empathy is a powerful tool in any argument, and disabled people need that empathy rather than sympathy. People have been fighting these fights for a very long time, and frequently disabled fights are isolated ones, ones where there is no grand compassion from the population as a whole to hold the fight up. I have been in discussion groups and on panels for so long, where the same faces are saying the same things to the same crowds. Because it does – and I would say the treatment of disabled people over the past 10 years backs this up – feel as though no one is listening. TV can help, and provide an understanding, so that when the next cuts come the marches don't just contain disabled people, and when the government pushes social care reform into the next parliament the response is righteous outrage from us all.

"The stories that we tell relegate disabled people to either victims or heroes."

At present, TV grossly underestimates disabled people, both in the stories that are told and the way they are told. I know these figures off by heart: 22% of this country are disabled, yet disabled talent makes up just 7.8% of the people we see onscreen. Even more disgracefully, disabled people make up just 5.2% of those behind the camera, and – when you get to the top – upsettingly, only 3.6% of all executives are disabled people. Twenty-two per cent of the population represented by only 3.6% in TV's governing class. Broadcasters have talked of the need to change this, and in 2017 Creative Diversity Network – a body that works with those broadcasters to increase inclusion – announced a target of doubling disability representation in front and behind the camera by 2021. But the CDN's interim report was damning; by 2020, the growth seen was only 0.9% in off-screen talent.

Meanwhile, the stories that we tell relegate disabled people to either victims or heroes. There is no nuance, no sophistication. The word "disabled" covers a whole range of different impairments, and – this feels so obvious but it is rarely reflected – a complete range of different personalities.

You wouldn't believe it watching TV. You get the acerbic disabled friend, or the hero desperately trying to run along a street using crutches. Disabled people on TV rarely have love lives, rarely have families even; they are denied the opportunity to be assholes, or flippant or weird. I'm not arguing for – block capitals – IMPORTANT television here or anything as dull as that. What I'm arguing for is good quality programming that includes disabled people and disabled stories.

TV needs to change, and it needs to change rapidly. We need to change the sort of people telling stories, we need to change the sort of stories that are told, and most crucially – and this is particular to disability – we need to change the spaces we tell the stories in. Because the majority of our studio spaces are still inaccessible. Which means disabled people can't work in them. I tell of a friend of mine in my speech who had to crawl her way to work across a muddy trailer, and how she had to restrict her use of the toilet – and therefore her food and drink intake – to once a day because the facilities were inaccessible. This is the tip of a very horrible iceberg.

I do not speak for all disabled people, and they wouldn't want me to, however I have been determined to in this case because change is overdue and it is necessary. We need serious reform and we need it fast. TV doesn't reflect our country and it needs to.

23 August 2021

Disability should be part of Black history conversations – I've gone my whole life seeing people like me erased

It was difficult growing up feeling like my identity was a massive taboo, even among people of the same ethnicity. Battling two barriers makes it double the challenge, writes Nana Marfo.

By Nana Marfo

Growing up black in Great Britain was very challenging for me in the 1990s, when representation felt perhaps as limited as it is today. Being a disabled boy too, I had double the challenge of being and felt my voice wasn't important enough – which, looking back, made me too hard to be recognised.

Living with a tracheostomy meant that my voice was very shallow and speaking for me was often difficult, making my presence vocally limited. Eager for acceptance, I'd often walk around with my tracheostomy tube visible to the naked eye; which often made people inquisitive and intrigued to know what it was.

It usually led to the sort of conversations that gave me a platform to express myself, talking about how I was born premature and what it meant to have a narrow airway. I've come far since then. In adulthood, I've gained the moniker "Mr Unique Voice", a man with a trachea tube which enables me to breathe and speak my truth of equality.

Growing up, it felt odd not being able to see many people who were black and disabled. I remember thinking society was ashamed of people who looked and sounded different.

People like me. Was I being punished due to my narrow airway? Was I not good enough?

And what were other black disabled people going through if I as a child at the time believed I wasn't worthy?

I never really saw people like myself on TV and frequently asked my mother why black people weren't equally represented as white people; from a young age of six, I felt we all needed to be given the same opportunities.

Talkative and full of questions, I wanted to know why I hardly saw people like me; or whether black people had been "naughty", seeing as we weren't, as I interpreted it, "allowed" to be on small or large screens across the nation. It was that curiosity that spurred my father on to educate me about my cultural heritage at the tender age of seven.

After having a harsh eye-opening lecture from him about our culture and what being black in Great Britain truly meant, my hunger to understand why and how black people came to this journey intensified. Though prominent figures such as BBC presenter Andi Peters and ITN's Trevor McDonald gave me a small glimpse of hope, by the time I became a teenager, I realised I felt miles apart from my peers and the wider black community due to being disabled.

Black disabled representation in the UK is still shockingly rare. But there are plenty of figures I wish we did a better job of celebrating. One of which is television presenter and wheelchair basketball player Ade Adepitan. Coming from Nigeria, where disability as a whole can in some arenas be seen as witchcraft, or evidence of the past sins of parents being punished by God, I've always seen Adepitan as uniquely inspirational.

He contracted polio as a baby, which caused complications to his mobility, losing sensation and movement in his left leg, making it difficult to walk. After moving to the United Kingdom, Adepitan did not allow his disability or his skin colour deem what he could and couldn't do. He would have been, as so many black disabled people are, fully aware that he had two separate barriers to contend with, but went on to accomplish great recognition in the 2004 summer Paralympics as well as the 2005 Paralympic world cup. Through the contributions of people like him, it was again proven to me that being black and disabled shouldn't be seen as the barrier it is often treated as.

Marsha de Cordova, shadow secretary of state for women and equalities, is another source of inspiration. Elected as the first black MP with a disability within the house of parliament in 2014 (Cordova was born with nystagmus and is registered blind), she works to fight for inclusion while working tirelessly to represent people within Battersea, her constituency. Watching this lady's achievements taught me an insightful lesson that no matter her impairment and struggles as a black woman, she didn't allow her impaired vision to hold her back.

I like to think I have the same approach to my life. It was difficult growing up feeling like the duality of my identity was a massive taboo (even among people of the same ethnicity) due to society's lack of understanding about disability and the far-reaching impacts of ableism. But it opened my eyes to the importance of doing what I do today. Not only is there a fight to be noticed as a black person but battling two barriers makes it double the challenge.

I see this while doing my advocacy work in the UK too. I am invited to speak on issues affecting black disabled communities on a regular basis, and through it, I've learned that there is an incredible lack of understanding from workplace policy, law enforcement, local authorities and more – all of which still have yet to figure out how to fairly work with and represent black disabled people.

Take the case of Osime Brown, a severely autistic 21-year-old man who is currently facing deportation to Jamaica, a country he hasn't been back to since he was 4 years-old, for example. Despite desperate pleas for compassion over his case, at each opportunity where he could have been supported, he seems, as far as I can see, to have been let down by the local authorities, the police and the educational system alike.

These failings may well have led him into being convicted for a crime he maintains he is innocent of. It's not a stretch in my view, given quotes from his mother, that he may not have even been fully aware of what was happening at the time because of his disability.

Even his behaviour since being incarcerated points to his vulnerability. He has been said to ring his mother to ask her if he needs to wash his hair, among other devastating examples. Still, this young man is facing deportation, with no demonstrable concern from the state and about his wellbeing.

Institutionally, the justice system has never been fair to black people. To be a disabled person in addition is a double punishment.

It's why I'm so thankful for voices like Olajumoke Abdullahi and Kym Oliver, campaigners who go by the name "The Triple Cripples", and seek to expose the fact that: "Disabled people are practically non-existent in mainstream media".

As they observe, if disabled people are largely absent from mainstraim spaces like these, "imagine how underrepresented Black and non-Black, women, femmes or non-binary people with disabilities are".

To have three reasons why you feel your voice and existence is not worthy and having to fight for equal and fair share of society's opportunities in 2020 shows you racism, sexism and ableism have long legacies that need to be rewritten.

There has been a massive awakening about the importance of giving marginalised groups a seat at the table this year but there's more work to be done. For disabled black Brits in particular, that workload is mountainous. If Black Lives Matter, disabled black lives should too. The sooner society wakes up to that, the more freedom we'll all be able to enjoy.

28 October 2020

Paralympics haven't decreased barriers to physical activity for most people with disabilities

An article from The Conversation.

THE CONVERSATION

By Kathleen A. Martin Ginis, Professor and Director of Centre for Chronic Disease Prevention and Management, University of British Columbia and Cameron M. Gee, Postdoctoral fellow at ICORD, University of British Columbia

More than 4,000 athletes from around the world will compete at the Tokyo Paralympic Games, a tenfold increase since the first Paralympics in 1960. Despite the growth in Paralympic athletes, for most of the world's 1.5 billion people with a disability, participation in sports, exercise and other types of physical activity is still nearly impossible.

In a recent research review, we reported that children, youth and adults with disabilities are up to 62 per cent less likely to meet the World Health Organization's physical activity guidelines than the general population. This is because people with disabilities face over 200 barriers to doing physical activity, two of the largest being built environments and transportation. For example, most public playgrounds, swimming pools, and outdoor tracks are built in ways that make them inaccessible to wheelchair users.

Accessibility is key

Even fitness and recreation facilities that say they are accessible often lack basic accessible features, such as changing rooms, showers and clear pathways so that a person with a visual or physical impairment can easily move about.

Truly accessible facilities are often underutilized. Worldwide, people with disabilities can't get to these places because they have limited or no access to public transit services.

Participation costs are another big barrier. People with disabilities are more likely to live in poverty. Some facilities demand additional entrance fees from family members who come along to help the person with a disability. Adapted sports equipment is expensive – a special wheelchair for playing wheelchair basketball can cost as much as $5,000.

Physical activity barriers create health inequities. Persons with disabilities are at greater risk for developing chronic diseases linked to physical inactivity, such as Type 2 diabetes and cardiovascular disease. They are also at greater risk for depression, anxiety and other mental health problems.

Some of the risk can be reduced by participating in sports, exercise and active play. Our recent research found that physical activity significantly improved the cardiometabolic health, physical fitness and mental health of children, youth and adults with disabilities.

Even small amounts of activity — well below the levels recommended by the World Health Organization — can improve health and well-being.

Inspiration does not equal participation

People with and without disabilities often say they feel inspired by watching Paralympic athletic performances. Unfortunately, the inspiration and sport enthusiasm created by the Paralympics (known as the "demonstration effect") has little effect on actual sport participation.

In 2012, more than 31 million television viewers across England watched the London Paralympic Games. And yet, from 2006 to 2016, the percentage of people with disabilities in England who participated in sport increased by just 1.5 per cent. Sport participation rates hit a high of 19.1 per cent of the disability population in 2013. By 2016, that number had fallen to just 16.8 per cent.

What happened? After the London Paralympics, British disability and sport organizations were not adequately resourced to support the influx of new participants. There was also a greater focus on getting people with disabilities to try a sport rather than addressing the barriers preventing them from staying in sport. Ultimately, the motivation created by the Paralympics was not enough to override the longstanding barriers to sport participation.

Pandemic launched new initiatives

The COVID-19 pandemic has created even more barriers to participation. Regions have locked down. Facilities and programs have closed. Access to personal support workers and other disability services has been lost. But there is a silver lining — these challenges have spurred some new actions.

Throughout the pandemic, organizations around the world have provided free online workout programs for people with physical and intellectual disabilities. Our research team with the Canadian Disability Participation Project launched a free physical activity coaching service for Canadians with disabilities. Coaches give information and motivation, by phone, to help clients overcome barriers to being active during the pandemic.

The province of Ontario recognized physical activity as being critical to the health of people with disabilities. Sports and recreational facilities were allowed to open during the province's shutdown so people with disabilities could do physical therapy.

While these efforts are encouraging, they must be part of a long-term, global solution.

International and national physical activity action plans note the importance of addressing the needs of people with disabilities. These action plans have not been given enough resources to make real change.

The Paralympics will raise awareness about sporting possibilities for people with disabilities. Some viewers may even be inspired to try a new sport, join a gym, or simply to go outside and play. Now is the time to move beyond the optics of the Paralympics and push for proper investment and serious action to remove the barriers to physical activity in our built environments, policies and communities and effect real change for people with disabilities.

22 August 2021

CBeebies announces new presenter George Webster to delighted reaction from viewers

Webster previously starred in a BBC Bitesize video dispelling myths about Down's Syndrome.

By Annabel Nugent

CBeebies have announced George Webster as a new guest presenter on CBeebies House – and viewers are thrilled.

The BBC children's channel revealed that Webster would be joining the show as a presenter in a Twitter post shared today (20 September).

"EXCITING NEWS. Our NEW CBeebies House presenter, George will be starting soon," reads the post. "He loves cooking and dancing, and he can't wait to be your friend."

The 20-year-old, who has Down's Syndrome, is an actor, dancer and ambassador for Mencap, a UK-based charity that works to improve the lives of people with learning difficulties.

Speaking about the announcement, Webster said: "I feel so proud and I'm feeling so excited to start!"

People took to Twitter with heartwarming responses to news of Webster's appointment.

"My boy has autism and he turned to me and said 'I like George Daddy.' That's all you need to know. Thank you CBEEBIES," wrote one user. "You've done a wonderful thing today."

Many people shared photographs of themselves and their children excited to watch Webster's debut as a presenter.

"Wonderful to have diversity on tv aimed at the next generation," wrote another. "As a mum of disabled children (teenagers now) this is so important to include everyone and produce acceptance of all."

A third person wrote: "CBeebies you have made a mum of a little boy just like George so excited. You are the best x."

"He's fantastic. I have a 5 year old George with DS and this brilliant lad made our day," said someone else.

Earlier this year, Webster starred in a BBC Bitesize video dispelling myths about Down's Syndrome.

In it, he said: "I'm George, I'm 20 years old and I have Down's Syndrome. I call myself George because that's who I am. Not Down's George."

"I have an amazing life," he added.

20 September 2021

Why investing in social care could boost the economy by helping disabled people be independent

Investment in social care could generate between £6 billion and £20 billion for the economy by helping disabled people into work, disability charity Leonard Cheshire reveals. To champion the life-changing and empowering impacts of social care, it is launching a new campaign, Care for Equality. Find out more and how you can get involved.

By Leonard Cheshire

If the government reforms social care it could boost the economy by £6 billion to £20 billion, including £1-4 billion in income tax.

Our new findings, based on economic modelling (see more on this below), show social care has the potential to pay for itself, with previous studies by The Health Foundation indicating an additional £2-12.2 billion is needed annually to bridge the social care funding gap.

More widely available social care would allow many disabled people to increase their income through entering work, progress existing careers or increase their working hours.

More importantly, it would empower disabled people to live their lives as they choose.

Hannah, 37, from Cheshire told the charity: "One of the biggest differences social care has made to me is independence. I can now socialise with friends and I have a job.

"I have achieved goals that I wouldn't have dreamed of a few years ago. I work two days each week at police headquarters. My care worker stays with me, so if I need anything they are there and ready to enable me."

Not everyone the charity spoke to currently benefits from such care, as Simon, 42, from Cambridgeshire revealed: "The lack of support I have received has not helped with my employment prospects.

"I would like to get some work experience or do some voluntary work to improve my skills and experience and therefore my overall employability prospects. But there is no support.

"There is Access to Work, but it has not managed to get me into actual employment because it only gives help to those already in paid work, not for those trying to improve their employability".

The government's focus to date has been making social care work for people aged 65 plus.

This is despite a third of all people who draw on social care being aged 18-64.

Our new campaign, Care for Equality, aims to highlight the empowering potential of social care for working-age disabled adults.

We're calling on the government to urgently invest in care and work with disabled people to ensure social care reforms offer them choices and personalised options, so it fully meets their needs. We're also asking the government to reform how care staff are paid and to fund training.

Disabled people told us that when they could get care tailored to their needs, they were able to "thrive" and not just "survive".

Our research also uncovered claims that current assessment processes lack an in-depth understanding of disabled people's lives. Individuals raised concerns to us about eligibility criteria for social care, with one person claiming she was told that she was "not disabled enough to have the social care support I wanted".

The pandemic was found to have disrupted many individuals' care, with reductions in the number of hours received and long waits for specialist equipment.

The charity's CEO, Ruth Owen OBE, said: "Economic arguments shouldn't be the reason to reform social care, but as our research shows, they should no longer be a barrier.

"We want the government to have serious conversations with disabled people about social care, so it can meet their needs and support their life aspirations.

"Social care isn't just about getting up and washed, though this kind of support is vital. It's also about people being able to see friends and family, being able to travel, have hobbies, have a job, or seek higher education.

"The current government isn't the first to kick the proverbial social care can down the road, but it needs to be the last. No more excuses, no more stalling – investing in care benefits everyone."

Leonard Cheshire Director of Policy Gemma Hope said: "Disabled people have a right to social care, so we look forward to hearing how the government will make it work better for everyone who needs it.

"So many of us will need the extra support social care can provide in our lifetime. It's in everyone's interests for social care reform to be delivered as a priority. The Autumn's Comprehensive Spending Review is an opportunity for some serious investment.

"This is about more than money though. Disabled people must be involved in how social care is reformed to ensure any new system offers choice and the chance for personcentered care. We hope that our new data is a wake-up call for the government."

Leonard Cheshire's Care For Equality campaign

Through our new campaign, Care For Equality, we're calling on policymakers in each country of the UK to create a social care system which fully meets the needs of disabled people.

The change we want to see:

♦   Ensure the social care system fully meets the needs of disabled people

♦   Engage and co-produce reforms with disabled people

♦   Invest in social care

♦   Build in greater choice and personalisation

♦   Increase funding for better workforce pay, training and career development

We're also asking the public to voice their support for urgent social care reform, to ensure equality for all. For more information about the #CareForEquality campaign and how to get involved please visit leonardcheshire.org/care-for-equality and join us on Twitter @leonardcheshire.

Our research and data

There are 3 main ways in which disabled people are economically disadvantaged:

1.   Disabled people who are in work earn about 12% less, on average, than non-disabled counterparts

2.   Disabled people who are currently looking for work are about twice as likely to be unemployed

3.   Many more disabled people are economically "inactive" (i.e., unemployed and not looking for a job) – they are about three times more likely to be inactive compared to the wider population

There are many reasons for these differences but unmet caring and support, which could be provided through improved social care, could help to reduce each of these three impacts.

Our analysis does not assume social care reform solves these three problems completely, but that reform helps to:

♦   Reduce the wage gap to the levels seen amongst the rest of the population

♦   Reduce unemployment of disabled people to the levels seen amongst the rest of the population

♦   Allow some of the inactive population of disabled people to seek work.

We have calculated that such improvements could boost the economy by £6 billion to £20 billion per year.

The top end of this range reflects the benefit of reducing the level of inactive disabled people (i.e., those not participating in the workforce) from about 43% to about 30%.

30% is still about twice as high as the level of inactivity amongst the wider population (i.e., it still assumes many disabled people cannot join the workforce for reasons beyond their support requirements).

Frontier Economics' modelling shows that reforming social care has the potential to pay for itself.

Previous research we have carried out shows there is not enough awareness of the scheme amongst employers: www.leonardcheshire.org/about-us/our-news/press-releases/disabled-workers-are-being-failed-employers.

27 July 2021

Why it makes good business sense to hire people with disabilities

An article from The Conversation.

By Catherine E. Connelly, Canada Research Chair and Professor of Organizational Behaviour, McMaster University and Sandra L. Fisher, Senior Research Fellow and Lecturer, Human Resource Management and Technology, Münster University of Applied Sciences

Managers sometimes assume that hiring employees who live with disabilities will be more expensive. They worry that these employees will perform at a lower level, be absent more often, need expensive accommodations and will then quit.

But should managers worry about these things?

We present a way for managers to evaluate both the net costs and benefits of having employees with disabilities, and we consider all these factors. When we tested our method at one company, we found that it actually saved money by hiring people with disabilities.

To calculate the net value of employing people with disabilities, companies can run what is known as a utility analysis that takes into account direct costs associated with wages, benefits, training and accommodation. It also considers indirect costs such as turnover and absences.

Direct costs are easily tabulated, but indirect costs are based on industry estimates.

For example, turnover costs can be estimated as one to 2.5 times the annual salary of the worker who leaves, depending on how lengthy the search is for a replacement and how much on-boarding is required. These costs are balanced against the value provided by the employees, taking into account employee performance evaluations and pay rates.

Disabled employees were more productive

A food services company that runs hospital cafeterias and university food courts allowed us to analyze their internal data for one department with 46 employees. Our analysis suggests that this unit had $108,381 in added value that year by hiring employees with disabilities.

The employees with disabilities at this company performed at a slightly higher level compared to their counterparts without disabilities. Only 56 per cent of the non-disabled employees had average or above-average performance, but all the employees with disabilities met this standard. Similarly, the non-disabled employees had an average of 6.5 absences per year, but workers with disabilities had an average of only three absences over the same time period.

At this company, the employees with disabilities also had much lower turnover. In fact, none of the employees with disabilities left the company during the year of our study. In contrast, 18 per cent of the non-disabled employees quit.

Managers sometimes believe in false stereotypes that employees with disabilities are unreliable and likely to quit, but in this company they were loyal and reliable. This is consistent with what we have learned from our conversations with managers at other companies.

Several managers gave us examples of employees with disabilities who were dedicated and committed workers once they had been given an opportunity and welcomed into the company. One chain restaurant executive, in particular, started hiring more workers with disabilities because he noticed that they were very unlikely to quit.

What might surprise some managers is that the costs of the accommodations for employees with disabilities were quite low. One employee, a chef, was deaf and could not hear food orders — so the counter staff would write them down for him. The company estimated that the cost of the paper and pens to do this was just five dollars.

Most of of the other employees with disabilities only needed some scheduling flexibility to deal with medical flareups or appointments. This was easily provided and these accommodations were similar to those provided to everyone else.

Providing accommodations

Naturally, employees hired by companies will have varying disabilities. Information on how to provide accommodations is available from a number of sources, including the Job Accommodation Network and local community organizations like the Gateway Association, the Canadian Council on Rehabilitation and Work, the Neil Squire Association and the March of Dimes. Businesses should also ask their employees what they need to be successful.

Although the accommodation costs in our example might sound unusually low, the typical costs of workplace accommodations tend to be lower than what managers expect. According to industry estimates, accommodations actually cost less than US$500 in nearly 60 per cent of cases, or about $625 in Canada.

Why? A company may offer modified duties or flexible schedules to employees with disabilities. These are generally not expensive to provide.

And in instances where there is a price tag for an accommodation — for example, an ergonomic mouse or standing desk — these are often one-time costs. More expensive investments, like wheelchair ramps, are rarer but can be amortized over several years.

Going beyond CSR

Many advocates for hiring people with disabilities focus on doing so to fulfil corporate social responsibility expectations. We agree that corporate social responsibility is important, but the financial component is critical to highlight to business leaders.

Companies can use their internal employee data to develop a plan that supports equity, diversity and inclusion efforts when it comes to people with disabilities.

Job applicants who live with disabilities represent a largely untapped sector of the workforce — unemployment rates among these workers tend to be about double that of non-disabled workers, with comparable age and education levels.

Managers who are seeking loyal employees who perform well should consider hiring people with disabilities. It's a smart business strategy.

8 August 2021

Disabled fashion designer bringing inclusive clothing brand to Cambridge

Unhidden will be the first adaptive clothing brand sold in Cambridge.

By Becca Field

Clothing designed for disabled people will be available in Cambridge as a brand new company moves into a city shopping centre.

Unhidden, an adaptive clothing brand that designs garments for disabled people, will host events that raise awareness of the need for inclusivity in the fashion industry as it moves into The Grafton Centre.

Unhidden will be in the shopping centre this coming Sunday (August 3) and every Sunday for the next three months.

The fashion brand has partnered with retail tech startup Sook to make them the first-ever adaptive clothing brand to be sold in Cambridge.

It has been been working to achieve inclusivity in the fashion industry since its launch in November of last year.

The founder and CEO of Unhidden, Victoria Jenkins, explained why clothing designed for disabled people was necessary and why the issue was close to her heart.

Victoria is a fashion industry veteran and was inspired to create Unhidden due to her own disabilities caused by gastrointestinal conditions.

She said: "I'm now a disability advocate and speaker, which I have only really taken to recently.

"It has absolutely been impacted by my journey.

"It was while I was in hospital in 2016 when I met a fellow patient who inspired me to start Unhidden.

"She had to take everything off every time the doctors came round.

"In general life, she could only really wear jogging bottoms and a t-shirt which mentally for her was not very fun and was still very restrictive."

From her own hospital bed Victoria began her research and what she found was disappointing.

She said the only adaptive clothing available "wasn't especially stylish, very elderly and medical looking."

This gave Victoria the inspiration to use all of her knowledge for a better cause and do something that helps others as "there are so many people who need it".

The clothes made by Unhidden aim to make life easier, more comfortable, and more fashionable for those with disabilities.

Some examples of how they achieve this includes making trousers specifically for wheelchair users which don't rise up when you sit down, and any excess material behind the knee has been removed to get rid of any bits of pressure on your body.

There are no seams or pockets as they can cause pressure sores on wheelchair users and a looser material makes it easier for carers to put on the trousers.

The looser material also means a catheter can be fed through parts of the trousers.

Unhidden has made shirts and dresses with openings that make it easier for people with diabetes or cancer to receive medicine.

The shirts can also be customised at checkout with magnetic fastenings so people with cerebral palsy don't have to spend time fiddling with buttons, which is also helpful for people with arthritis and stroke patients.

Victoria said that mainstream fashion isn't inclusive enough and is failing to represent the 14.1 million disabled people in the UK.

She said: "I didn't realise how much I would've benefited from adaptive design as I'd just never heard of it before.

"I studied fashion design and it's never covered and is still very rare for it to be covered now.

"If we're not talking to fashion designers about inclusive design when they're studying and learning about it then it will be very difficult for it to become standard and normalised.

"Adaptive clothing is the last fashion of the fashion revolution, inclusive design is very lacking in this country."

Victoria added: "One in five people have a disability and the UK high-street loses £267 million a month by not being accessible.

"But also because they don't have products that are specifically targeted at people with disabilities.

"We're not very represented as it is, we have something like two to three per cent coverage in media globally, which given that we're actually 50 per cent of the world's population is not ideal.

"What I'm trying to do with Unhidden is get positive representation and show fashion can be fun and should be fun and can be something everyone can enjoy."

Victoria also has plans to hosts talks about adaptive design and ableism, about which she wrote a book earlier in the year called The Little Book of Ableism.

It aims to act as a guide on language and allyship to the disabled community.

These talks aim to highlight the barriers that people with disabilities face on a day-to-day basis.

Unhidden was the first adaptive clothing brand to appear in London and on Sunday will also be a first for Cambridge.

At The Grafton Centre this weekend, there will also be charities they support including Not a Phase and Models of Diversity who promote equality and diversity for disabled people.

Unhidden was founded in 2016 and launched in November of last year, making it the accumulation of four years of research and development.

6 August 2021

Nike launches hands-free shoes inspired by man with cerebral palsy

Nike has launched the GO FlyEase, accessible hands-free shoes that are easy to put on and take off by simply slipping your foot in without bending down to do up laces, zips or straps.

By Emma Purcell

The innovative design was inspired by Matthew Walzer, who wrote a letter at age 16 to Nike asking for an accessible pair of shoes he could put on and off independently because he has cerebral palsy.

Following nine years of researching, engineering and testing, the GO FlyEase hands-free shoe is now launched and will be available to purchase soon.

How do the Nike GO FlyEase hands-free shoes work?

The Nike GO FlyEase hands-free shoes are a sophisticated and accessible way of wearing footwear. Behind the shoe's smooth motion is a bi-stable hinge that enables the shoe to be secure in fully-open and fully-closed positions.

This duality allows another signature detail: the Nike GO FlyEase tensioner. The tensioner's unique flexibility super-charges an action many might take for granted (kicking-off a shoe) and completely reimagines this movement as the basis for an accessible and empowering design.

Not only will the GO FlyEase shoes be life-changing and gain further independence to disabled people, but the hands-free shoes will also benefit the wider community, including professional athletes, pregnant women, parents with their hands full and students late for classes.

Matthew Walzer's campaign for hands-free shoes

The creation of the GO FlyEase hands-free shoe was inspired by Matthew Walzer, a young man with cerebral palsy from Florida, USA.

In 2012, at the age of 16, he wrote a letter to Nike requesting a pair of shoes that he would not have to tie laces on or do up straps due to his dexterity issues.

At the time, Matthew was pursuing university and wanted to be able to put on his shoes and take them off unassisted so that he could live independently.

Matthew was two months premature and had underdeveloped lungs, which led to his cerebral palsy diagnosis. Doctors told his parents that he would never walk, but he has proved them wrong. He also never developed an expected speech impediment and was a strong student.

He said: "At 16 years old, I was able to completely dress myself, but my parents still had to tie my shoes. As a teenager who was striving to become totally self-sufficient, I found this extremely frustrating, and at times, embarrassing,"

When sending the letter, Matthew never expected a response from Nike: "I knew what I was doing was, in football terms, 'a Hail Mary,' and to be quite honest I had very low expectations.

I was expecting a very polite letter back in recognition of my request. There are not enough 'thank yous' in the world to express my undying gratitude".

Further than this, Matthew got to collaborate with Nike designer Tobie Hatfield to create the GO FlyEase and a few months after sending his letter, Matthew got to test the first prototype of the hands-free shoes.

"Your talented team of designers has thoughtfully created a shoe that, for the first time in my life, I can put on myself.

"When I put the shoes on every morning, they give the greatest sense of independence and accomplishment I have ever felt in my life," said Matthew at the time.

About a week ago, Matthew was sharing his story on radio station NPR ahead of the GO FlyEase launch, and when he was asked if the shoes were cool, he replied:

"I haven't tried them yet. I don't have a pair yet. So, from what I've seen online, they are.

"They do look extremely cool. And I'm very, very excited to try them."

The benefits of hands-free shoes for Paralympic athletes

These new accessible shoes are also likely to benefit Paralympic athletes, including champion fencer Bebo Vio.

Bebo lost both her arms and legs to meningitis as a child and competes in a wheelchair and walks using prosthetic legs. Putting on her shoes is usually a time-consuming activity.

"With the Nike Go FlyEase, I just need to put my feet in and jump on it. The shoes are a new kind of technology, not only for adaptive athletes but for everyone's real life," she says.

How to buy GO FlyEase hands-free shoes

The hands-free shoes are expected to be priced at £104.95 and available in three styles:

- Anthracite, Racer Blue and black

- Celestine Blue, Volt and white

- Dynamic Turquoise, Hyper Crimson and black

The Nike GO FlyEase is available initially via invite for select Nike Members on Monday 15th February 2021, with "broader consumer" availability planned for later this year.

Greeper shoelaces

If you don't fancy purchasing a new pair of shoes but have difficulty tying laces because of mobility or dexterity issues, then the Greeper shoelaces may be your answer.

Sold on the Disability Horizons Shop, the Greeper shoelaces are a modern, accessible alternative to traditional shoelaces – they remain tight and tied no matter what conditions they're put under.

These innovative shoelaces have been designed to aid those with disabilities to adapt any type of everyday shoe, without having to rely on old-fashioned velcro fastening shoes.

There are three styles of Greeper shoelaces available – sport laces, hiking laces and Thomas the Tank Engine laces for children.

In addition, there is a Greeper Assist, which is an aid that helps tighten Greeper shoelaces with just one hand.

For more information about Greeper shoelaces and the Greeper Assist, check out Zec Richardson's review on the Disability Horizons Shop. To find out more about Greeper shoelaces plus other adapted clothing available, visit the Disability Horizons Shop.

12 February 2021

Key Facts

- According to the World Report on Disability, the number of people with disabilities is increasing. This is because populations are ageing (older people have a higher risk of disability) and because of the global increase in chronic health conditions associated with disability, such as diabetes, cardiovascular diseases and mental illness. (page 2)

- It is estimated that worldwide about one in 160 children has an ASD. (page 3)

- There are 14.1 million disabled people in the UK, that's 1 in 5 people. (page 6)

- 60% of people in the UK underestimate how many disabled people there actually are. (page 7)

- 49% of working age adults feel excluded from society because of their condition or impairment. (page 7)

- More than half (53%) of the 196 people who responded to a survey carried out by Leonard Cheshire said they have experienced hate crime in a public place in the past three years, with 32 people seeing them happening during the coronavirus pandemic. (page 16)

- Leonard Cheshire also conducted research with fellow charity United Response. They found that reports of disability hate crime are up 12% across 36 regions in England and Wales in 2019/20 but only 1.6% of cases resulted in police charging the perpetrators. (page 18)

- The number of people with a learning disability who died this year in England and Wales (not in hospitals or the community but in care settings alone) was up by 134% compared to the same period in 2019. This is a preliminary and conservative estimate. (page 24)

- Local councils have lost nearly £16 billion in core funding since 2010, equating to 60%. By 2025, the Local Government Association estimates that adult social care in England and Wales alone faces a deficit of £3.5 billion. (page 24)

- A new study, partly carried out by the ONS, estimated that, in England, between 24 January 2020 and 28 February 2021, 105,213 people died from causes involving Covid-19, of whom 61,000 were disabled. That's almost 60% of all deaths. (page 28) 22% of this country are disabled, yet disabled talent makes up just 7.8% of the people we see onscreen. Even more disgracefully, disabled people make up just 5.2% of those behind the camera, and – when you get to the top – upsettingly, only 3.6% of all executives are disabled people. (page 28)

- Recent research shows that children, youth and adults with disabilities are up to 62 per cent less likely to meet the World Health Organization's physical activity guidelines than the general population. (page 30)

- In 2012, more than 31 million television viewers across England watched the London Paralympic Games. And yet, from 2006 to 2016, the percentage of people with disabilities in England who participated in sport increased by just 1.5 per cent. Sport participation rates hit a high of 19.1 per cent of the disability population in 2013. By 2016, that number had fallen to just 16.8 per cent. (page 31)

- Social care reforms could boost the economy by £6 billion to £20 billion, including £1-4 billion in income tax. (page 33)

- Disabled people who are in work earn about 12% less, on average, than non-disabled counterparts. (page 34)

Accessibility

Accessibility is a measure to assess how user-friendly or inclusive something is to specific groups of people. Something can be accessible to some people while being inaccessible to others.

Autism spectrum disorders

Autism spectrum disorders (ASDs) are a group of developmental disabilities that can cause social, communication and behavioural challenges. ASDs includes several conditions that used to be diagnosed separately: autistic disorder, pervasive developmental disorder not otherwise specified (PDD-NOS), and Asperger's syndrome. These conditions are now all called autism spectrum disorder.

Blue badge

A Blue Badge provides parking concessions for people with disabilities allowing them or their driver to park closer to their destinations. The permit can be used in any vehicle, as long as the badge holder is present (whether driving or being driven). It isn't assigned to a specific vehicle.

Disability

The Equality Act 2010 defines a disabled person as anyone who has a physical or mental impairment that has a substantial and long-term adverse affect on his or her ability to carry out day-to-day activities (NHS Choices, 2012). The nature of the disability will determine the extent to which it impacts on an individual's daily life. The definition of disability includes both physical impairments, such as multiple sclerosis or blindness, and learning disabilities such as autism.

Discrimination

Discrimination is the unjust or prejudicial treatment of of a group of people based on certain characteristics, such as disability.

Learning disability

A learning disability is a reduced intellectual ability to understand new or complex information and learn new skills, causing difficulty in carrying out everyday tasks. A learning disability can be mild, moderate or severe.

Non-visible disability

A non-visible disability is a disability that isn't immediately apparent. This includes conditions such as: autism, arthritis, mental health issues, diabetes, dementia, epilepsy and cystic fibrosis.

Paralympic Games

The Paralympic Games are a series of sporting competitions open to athletes with a wide range of disabilities. They are held immediately following the Olympic Games.

Social care

Social care is a network of services that provide support to people with learning disabilities, physical disabilities, illnesses and mental illnesses. Social care is provided in many different forms ranging from household help, to personal care, to help accessing specialist equipment or residential care. Social care is either provided formally through council or private fund or informally through family members, friends or neighbours.

Activities

Brainstorming

♦ Brainstorm what you know about disability.

- What types of disability are there?

- What do you understand by the term autism spectrum disorder?

- What types of discrimination do people with disabilities face?

- Give some examples of 'hidden' or non-visible disabilities.

Research

♦ Do some research into the different types of disability that exist. You should consider both physical and mental disabilities. Share your findings with the class.

♦ In pairs, research accessibility for disabled people when attending concert or theatre venues. You should consider what problems they face and what efforts have been made by the venues to help improve accessibility. Write a short report on your findings.

♦ In small groups, do some local research into support services that are available to people with disabilities, and their carers, living in your area. Make a list of what you have found that is available and a list of what you think should be available but isn't.

♦ Do some online research into autism and consider the following:

- which age groups this condition affects

- if one sex is more affected than another

- the different ways in which autism can present itself

Design

♦ In pairs, design a wheelchair friendly concert or theatre venue. It should be a friendly and safe place to visit.

♦ Choose one of the articles from this book and create an illustration that highlights the key themes of the piece.

♦ In pairs, design a sign to be displayed in a sports stadium directing disabled people to the areas which they can easily access.

♦ Choose a national disability charity and create a poster to raise awareness and encourage donations to the cause.

Oral

♦ Have a class discussion about the lack of disabled toilets on trains. Consider how you might feel if you were disabled and there were no working facilities available to you. What do you think should be done to overcome this?

♦ In small groups, compile a list of celebrities or people in the public eye who have a learning disability, physical disability or autism. Discuss reasons why people with disabilities are less visible in our society and media and what can be done to increase representation.

♦ In pairs stage a discussion between two work colleagues. A new member of staff has been taken on who is disabled. Talk about how this makes you feel and what improvements need to be made to make your workplace more inclusive and considerate to your new colleague's needs.

♦ Read the article on page 10: *Neglected, hidden away, registered dead: the tragic true story of the Queen's disabled cousins*. As a class, discuss how attitudes towards disability and the treatment of people with disabilities have changed over the years.

Reading/writing

♦ Write a one-paragraph definition of disability and include summaries of the following:

- The Social Model of Disability

- The Medical Model of Disability

♦ Imagine you are a young school student who has to care for a disabled family member. Write a letter to your MP describing what life is like on a daily basis for you. Make suggestions about what the government could do to improve quality of life for you and your disabled relative.

♦ Suggested reading:

- The Curious Incident of the Dog in the Night-Time - Mark Haddon

- The Reason I Jump - Naoki Higashida

- Crippled - Frances Ryan

- Wonder - R.J. Palacio

Acknowledgements

Images

Cover image courtesy of iStock. All other images courtesy of Freepik and Unsplash.

Illustrations

Simon Kneebone: pages 6, 16 & 22. Angelo Madrid: pages 9, 19 & 25.

Additional acknowledgements

With thanks to the Independence team: Shelley Baldry, Danielle Lobban and Jackie Staines.

Tracy Biram

Cambridge, September 2021